ABC's of Camp Cooking

I0737572

Virginia Clark

the call of the road
is a haunting sound—
the need to explore
to know
what made the land
as it is now
so long ago.
to see the land
that has seen such change,
and yet, not so.
it's a land that beckoned
so many men
to the golden lode,
now beckons us for
the beauty and
wonder
each turn
of the road.

P.O. Box 2485, Lake Havasu City, Arizona, 86405

ISBN 13: 978-0-931532-29-9
ISBN 10: 0-931532-29-9

ABC's of Camp Cooking Contents

Contents by Category

Breakfast

Soups, Salads and Sandwiches

Appetizers

Main Dishes

Main Dishes, cont.

Sides

Sides, cont.

Desserts

Beverages

Introduction

One of the great pleasures of camping is cooking in the out-of-doors within beautiful surroundings. Whatever your mode of travel, whether it be backpacking in the high altitude, camping in a tent, pop-up trailer, camper, travel trailer, motor home or boating the closeness to nature is rewarding. The wonderful aroma of campfire smoke, the vista of a lake, stream and mountains, the animals and birds close at hand, and the smell of evergreens enhance the experience. The dry desert camping among smoke trees with lizards scurrying around is satisfying also.

To ensure a good experience is to plan. Think out what your needs are, how much to take—the minimum—and make lists so the necessities are not forgotten. To camp in a motor home, trailer or pop-up the choices are easier than traveling with everything on your back. The size of the pantry is the determining factor in what and how much you can take.

"O is for On-the-Trail" chapter will give the backpacker ideas for traveling and cooking in the high altitude backcountry. Check "W is for Water Camping" chapter for suggestions and ideas on rafting, house boats and party-boat river and lake camping.

The sports that have become very popular are river rafting and camping with a houseboat or party-boat. The rafters use sand bars along the river to camp and explore while the houseboat and party-boat devotees cook and eat in the boat or onshore.

Shopping when traveling is fun as there are so many local foods in each part of the country—fresh fruits and vegetables at Farmers Markets, salmon and crab in Alaska, apples in Washington, potatoes in Idaho, herbs in Oregon, strawberries and vegetables in the California coastal region with fruit in the San Joachim Valley. There is beef in Nebraska, cheese in Wisconsin and Vermont, maple syrup and fish in New England, wine in New York, lobster and blueberries in Maine, corn in Kansas, seafood in the Atlantic Seaboard states, peaches in Georgia, citrus fruit in Florida, pecans and sweet potatoes in the South.

Remember the weather is not always warm and ideal. Prepare for some inclemency when planning. If you have enough room in the pantry stock up on soups and canned foods, crackers and cheese.

Most of the recipes are for a family of four or five and some are for individual servings. The emphases is on wholesome, easy foods, with interesting ideas you might enjoy. No exotic greens, overly hot or spicy foods. Always take an extra day's food supply for emergencies. It is better to be over prepared than to go hungry when you are held up somewhere.

Cooking Tips

1. A dash of salt in the oil when frying fish gives a better taste.
2. Do not overcook smoked fish or use too much heat as it will destroy the flavor.
3. Thaw frozen fish in milk to eliminate the frozen fish taste.
4. Do not overcook grilled fish as it will become dry and tough.
5. Keep oil from canned fish to sauté onions or other vegetables.
6. Mix fish oil with lemon juice and pepper to make a delicious salad dressing.
7. Rub lemon juice over fish before cooking. It will keep the fish white and prevent it from falling apart.
8. When boiling fish add some vinegar or lemon juice to the water.
9. Egg whites have greater volume when beaten at room temperature.
10. Cover egg yolks with cold water. They will stay fresh for days.
11. A cube of sugar in olive oil keeps oil from becoming rancid.
12. Fresh parsley in a screw-top jar in the refrigerator. It will keep about 3 weeks.
13. When mixing salad dressing stir seasoning in vinegar, then oil.
14. To keep celery crisp, place in cold water with a slice of potato.
15. Use onions flakes or powdered onion if you do not have fresh.
16. When food is too salty add potato to reduce the salt.

About the Author

I started to cook when I was in high school some seventy years ago. I peeled the potatoes, nightly, helped my sister prepare the vegetables and the roast. We were a family of seven. Our family was never heavy on desserts, but we had basic wholesome food. My Mother was known for her baked beans, apple pie and potato salad. Grandma Dean was well known for her sweet pickle relish which I tried to emulate but never could.

When I lived in the Village in New York City I was introduced to ethnic dishes from my many bohemian friends. I worked in the Food Section of the San Francisco Chronicle and learned about western and seafood dishes that I had not experienced in the East. I went down the John Muir Trail on horseback for my honeymoon and was up in the high country for six weeks. I learned to cook with dehydrated foods and ate lots of trout. The tall skyscrapers of steel and cement of New York were no match for the 11,000' elevation mountain passes. That was a great experience.

With three children we have traveled with campers, tents and trailers all over the United States, Canada and Mexico. We enjoy camping, fishing and cooking out of doors. I have written five cookbooks, and along with my husband, before he passed away, eight travel guides of the Sierra Nevada region. I hope you like the ssuggestions and recipes in this book and find something special to enjoy.

Contributers

Thanks to the following friends for their recipes and support:

Esther Chumbley, Lake Havasu City, Arizona
Sue Clagg, Arroyo Grande, California
Lewis Dean Clark, Camarillo, California
Margaret Clark, Flagstaff, Arizona
Hannah Dean, Brodhead, Wisconsin
Jean Miller Dean, Schenectady, New York
Linda Dean, Brodhead, Wisconsin
Logan Dean, Brodhead, Wisconsin
Paige and Matthew Dean, Greer, South Carolina
Phil Dirks, Lake Havasu City, Arizona
Heather Fanshawe, Queensland, Australia
Edna and Alec Farquharson, Kamloops, B. C., Canada
Marion Freisatz, Guilderland, New York
Fowler, Mama, Cariboo, B.C., Canada
Elizabeth Gattenby, Lake Havasu, Arizona
Betty Hommerding, Escondido, California
Neva Kelsey, Redding, California
Eloise Knowland, Seattle, Washington
Clara Lasselle, Guilderland, New York
Chang Lee, San Francisco, California
Ian and Audrey MacKenzie, Kamloops, B.C. Canada
Marjorie Mikesell, Eugene, Oregon
Wendy Sara-May Miller, Peoria, Arizona
Maggie Parker, Lake Havasu City, Arizona
Diane Pulasky, Lake Havasu City, Arizona
Wanda Smith, Lake Havasu City, Arizona
Mary Lou Teetsel, Guilderland, New York
Nancy Valenti, Lake Havasu City, Arizona

Also thanks to William Clark for assistance and support. And thanks to Bruce Fischer of Golden West Publishers for his assistance in presenting this book.

A is for Appetizers

Spicy Chips

2 FLOUR TORTILLAS
Butter-flavored COOKING SPRAY
½ tsp. each GARLIC POWDER, CUMMIN
 and CHILI POWDER
PARMESAN CHEESE

Cut tortillas into 8 wedges. Place on a baking sheet. Coat wedges with spray. Combine remaining ingredients. Mix well. Sprinkle evenly over wedges. Bake in 350-degree oven for 12 minutes or until crisp. Recipe can be doubled.

Crab or Clam Dip

1 8-oz. pkg. CREAM CHEESE, softened
¼ cup SOUR CREAM
1 Tbsp. LEMON JUICE
1 clove GARLIC, minced
1 Tbsp. GREEN ONION, thinly sliced
SALT to taste
½ lb. flaked CRAB or CLAM MEAT

Beat together cream cheese and sour cream. Add lemon juice, garlic, green onion and salt. Mix well. Add crab or clam meat. Cover and chill for 2 hours to blend flavors. This is good with crackers, celery strips or chips.

Clark's Family Favorite Appetizer Tray

Arrange cut-up bite-size pieces of sliced HAM or sliced BOLOGNA on a tray. Add bite-size pieces of SHARP CHEDDAR and SWISS CHEESE. Arrange sweet and crunchy PICKLES on the tray with RITZ CRACKERS. Make a sandwich and enjoy

Spinach Dip

1 10-oz. pkg. frozen chopped SPINACH, thawed and drained
1 8-oz. low-fat YOGURT
½ tsp. DILL WEED, crushed
½ tsp. ONION POWDER

Press the spinach between your hands to squeeze out all liquid. In a medium-size bowl mix the spinach with yogurt, dill weed and onion powder. Cover and chill until ready to use. This dip is very tasty with vegetables or crackers.

8-Layer Mexican Dip

1 14.5-oz. can REFRIED BEANS
½ lb. cool, cooked GROUND BEEF, crumbled
1 cup GUACAMOLE
1 cup SOUR CREAM
½ cup CHUNKY SALSA
1 4-oz. can DICED GREEN CHILI
1 2-oz. can BLACK OLIVES, sliced
1 cup shredded SHARP CHEDDAR CHEESE
1 chopped TOMATO
Strips of GREEN PEPPER

Spread the refried beans evenly at the bottom of a large open bowl or 9" pie plate. Cover with crumbled, cooked ground beef. Cover with guacamole. Cover the guacamole completely with sour cream so it doesn't brown. Make layers with salsa, green chilies, black olives and cheese. Garnish with tomatoes and green pepper. Chill. Serve with tortilla chips.

Marinated Herring

Place herring pieces from the jar on a cocktail cracker or buttered bread topped with onion rings and chopped dill.

Deviled Eggs

Submitted by Neva Kelsey, Redding, California

1 dozen HARD-COOKED EGGS, shelled and halved
1 can DEVILED HAM
Sprinkling of TABASCO SAUCE, PAPRIKA and
GROUND PEPPER
1 cup MAYONNAISE
1 Tbsp. VINEGAR

Scoop yellow yolks from egg. In a bowl mash, with a fork, a mixture of egg yolks with the rest of the ingredients. It should be thick. Spoon into egg cradles. Sprinkle with a little bit of paprika on the top. Place on deviled egg plate. Fill the center with pieces of cheese cubes or green and black olives for a relish tray.

Vegetable Dip

1 cup PLAIN YOGURT
½ cup COTTAGE CHEESE, softened
1 Tbsp. finely chopped GREEN PEPPER
3 Tbsp. finely chopped RED ONION
1 Tbsp. finely grated CARROT
1/8 tsp. GARLIC POWDER

Mix all ingredients together until smooth. Cover and chill. This is a delicious dip for broccoli, cauliflower bunches or crackers.

Sausage Cheese Chips

½ lb. KIELBASA, fully cooked
36 TORTILLA CHIPS
½ shredded MONTEREY JACK CHEESE
1 4-oz. can GREEN CHILI, chopped

Coarsely chop kielbasa. Set aside. Arrange tortilla chips on a greased 12" pizza pan. Mix kielbasa and cheese together. Sprinkle over chips. Spread chilies over all. Bake in 375-degree oven until cheese melts.

B is for Barbecue

Barbecue Sauce

2 cups KETCHUP
2 cups VINEGAR
1 5-oz. bottle WORCESTERSHIRE SAUCE
1 Tbsp. dried, chopped ONION
1 Tbsp. HOT SAUCE
1 Tbsp. BROWN SUGAR
1 Tbsp. SALT
1 cup BUTTER
2 cloves GARLIC, chopped
SALT and PEPPER to taste

Combine all ingredients in a medium-size saucepan. Bring to a boil and then simmer for 10 minutes. Makes 3 cups of sauce.

Butte Barbecue Chicken

Brush favorite barbecue sauce over chicken pieces. Grill over hot coals for 20 minutes for small pieces like wings, but longer for larger pieces like thighs. Turn chicken several times while cooking, brushing with the sauce. When chicken is cooked over hot coals the heat instantly seals in all the juices.

Bridgeport Hamburgers

1 lb. GROUND BEEF
½ cup HERBED BREAD CRUMBS
½ small ONION, chopped
SALT and PEPPER to taste
BARBECUE SAUCE

Combine all ingredients, except barbecue sauce. Form into patties. In a skillet slowly brown the patties for 15 minutes, turning once. Spread barbecue sauce over the patties. Cook 15 minutes more.

Barbecue Ham Steak

1 1½" -3" HAM STEAK
2 tsp. DRY MUSTARD
1 cup tightly packed BROWN SUGAR
½ cup ORANGE JUICE
½ cup SOUR CREAM

Remove any thick rind on the ham. Combine mustard, brown sugar and orange juice together. Place the ham over medium hot coals. Baste with the sauce. Turn and baste while cooking 3 or 4 times. Cook for about 20 minutes or until done.

Texas-Style Barbecue Sauce

1 large ONION chopped
2 cloves GARLIC, crushed
2 tsp. LEMON ZEST
Juice of 1 LEMON
½ cup CHILI SAUCE
½ cup RED WINE VINEGAR
1 Tbsp. WORCESTERSHIRE SAUCE
½ tsp. HOT PEPPER SAUCE
½ tsp. CHILI POWDER
SALT and PEPPER to taste

Combine all ingredients in a medium-size saucepan. Simmer for 15 minutes. Refrigerate until ready to use. Great for pork or beef. Chicken, too, if you like it hot. Baste the meat while cooking.

Herbed Barbecue Sauce for Poultry

Simmer for 30 minutes a cup of dry WHITE WINE, ¼ cup OLIVE OIL, 2 Tbsp. BUTTER, 1 Tbsp. DRIED ONIONS, 1 crushed clove of GARLIC, ½ tsp. SALT and ¼ tsp. PAPRIKA, 1 tsp. MINCED PARSLEY and 2 tsp. ROSEMARY.

Barbecue Sauce for Pork or Beef Ribs

½ cup LEMON JUICE
¼ cup HONEY
2 Tbsp. VEGETABLE OIL
1 Tbsp. KETCHUP
½ tsp. SALT
¼ tsp. OREGANO LEAVES
6 drops RED PEPPER SAUCE
2 cloves GARLIC, finely chopped
PORK or BEEF RIBS

Mix all ingredients together except the ribs. Cook to boiling. Cover and simmer for 10 minutes. Cool. Pour the sauce over the ribs. Marinate for 3 hours or overnight. Place ribs on grill. Turn and baste with the sauce while cooking.

Kentucky Barbecue Sauce

Submitted by Margaret Clark, Flagstaff, Arizona

1 cup KETCHUP
¼ cup RED WINE VINEGAR
¼ cup MOLASSES
1/3 cup KENTUCKY BOURBON
2 cloves GARLIC, crushed
2 tsp. SOY SAUCE
1 Tbsp. WORCESTERSHIRE SAUCE
1 Tbsp. LEMON JUICE
½ tsp. DRY MUSTARD
SALT and PEPPER to taste

Mix all ingredients in a bowl. Chill in refrigerator. Use with either beef or pork. Marinate at least for 2 hours. Yields 2 cups. When making, double the recipe and keep it in a jar in the refrigerator for future use.

C is for Chicken and Turkey

Chicken Foil Packs

Submitted by Clara Lasselle, Guilderland, New York

"Try them, as they are fun and there is no clean-up."

12 pieces FOIL SQUARES
6 Tbsp. MARGARINE
6 CHICKEN QUARTERS
6 medium POTATOES, sliced
6 CARROTS, sliced
2 or 3 ONIONS, peeled and sliced
SALT and PEPPER to taste
1 12-oz. bottle favorite BARBECUE SAUCE
WATER

Cut foil squares 18" long. Spread a tablespoon of margarine on 6 squares. Place chicken on each. Place potatoes, carrots and onion over the chicken. Add seasoning. Pour barbecue sauce over the vegetables. Sprinkle with water. Fold foil with the food tightly into packs. Rewrap each in second piece of foil.

Place packs directly on a bed of coals. Cook 45 minutes, turning once or twice with tongs. Unwrap and check one foil pack to see if it is done. If chicken needs more cooking, rewrap and cook longer.

Easy Creamed Turkey or Chicken

In a saucepan mix a10.5-oz. can CREAM OF CHICKEN SOUP with a cup of MILK. Add ¼ cup each chopped ONION and CELERY. Cook until tender. Add 2 cups cut-up cooked TURKEY or CHICKEN, ½ of 4-oz. can MUSHROOMS and SALT and PEPPER to taste. Heat thoroughly. Add ½ cup shredded SWISS or MONTEREY JACK CHEESE. Simmer until cheese is melted. Serve on heated flavored CROUTONS or TOAST.

Oriental Chicken

1 4-lbs. CHICKEN, cut up into pieces
1 20-oz.can PINEAPPLE CHUNKS
2 CARROTS, thinly sliced
1 small ONION, thinly sliced
2 stalks CELERY, thinly sliced
3 Tbsp. RED WINE VINEGAR
1 Tbsp. SOY SAUCE
½ tsp. DRY MUSTARD
SALT and PEPPER to taste
¾ cup sliced MUSHROOMS
2 GREEN PEPPERS, cut in strips
2 Tbsp. CORNSTARCH
2 Tbsp. WATER

Place chicken pieces, skin side up, in a skillet. Surround with pineapple chunks, carrots, onion and celery. Mix pineapple juice from the can with the vinegar, soy sauce and seasonings. Pour over chicken and vegetables. Add mushrooms and pepper strips. Combine cornstarch and water. Stir into liquid with the chicken. Cook over medium heat on top of the stove until chicken is done and liquid is bubbly and thickened. It can also be cooked in a 350-degree oven for 1 hour or until chicken is done.

Gunnison Chicken Marsala

1 4-5 lb. CHICKEN, cut up into pieces
2 Tbsp. MARGARINE
2 Tbsp. FLOUR
1 cup MILK
¼ tsp. CELERY SALT
1/8 tsp. PEPPER
5 MUSHROOMS. sliced
½ cup MARSALA

Arrange chicken pieces at the bottom of a skillet. Melt the butter in a small saucepan. Stir in flour, milk, seasonings, mushrooms and wine. Pour over the chicken. Cook in the skillet over medium heat for 45-50 minutes or until chicken pieces are cooked.

Hobo Chicken

Submitted by Diane Pulaskey, Lake Havasu City, Arizona

Make a big aluminum foil square for each person. Spray each square with vegetable non-stick spray. Lay 1 or 2 pieces of CHICKEN per person in the middle of the square, skin side down. Drain cans of VEGETABLES (green beans, peas, mixed vegetables, corn or carrots (2 each, whatever you prefer) and spread them over the chicken. Drain a can of SLICED POTATOES and place over the vegetables. Using about ½ can per person, spread CREAM OF CHICKEN SOUP over potatoes. Sprinkle with SALAD SEASONING over all. Draw up sides of foil squares and bind very tightly so they do not leak.

The chicken pouches can be cooked on a campfire with a grate, charcoal grill or oven. Do not place directly over fire but set pouches around the outside. Turn the pouches with tongs about every 10 minutes. Cook about 45 minutes to 1 hour. Eat right out of opened pouches. Put pouches on paper plates as the juice may leak. Be sure to have a spoon handy for the sauce. Mmmm good.

Baked Chicken

Submitted by Neva Kelsey, Redding, California

"This is a delicious chicken dish if you have a microwave, or cook it in a skillet on top of the stove, or in a Dutch oven."

Break apart one whole CHICKEN or use CHICKEN PIECES. Place in a baking dish or skillet with a cover. Mix 1 pkg. DRY ONION SOUP with a 10.5-oz. can of CREAM OF MUSHROOM SOUP. Mix the soups with MILK or WATER. Pour over chicken. Bake in a 350-degree oven for 1 hour, or until chicken is tender.

Hunter-Style Chicken

1 4-lb. CHICKEN, cut up into pieces
SALT and PEPPER to taste
FLOUR
OLIVE OIL
1 chopped GREEN PEPPER
2 medium ONIONS, chopped
1 large stalk CELERY, thinly sliced
1 clove GARLIC, chopped
1 14.5-oz can DICED TOMATOES
1 cup chopped MUSHROOMS

Prepare chicken and seasonings. Roll pieces in flour. Heat oil in a large skillet. Brown chicken on all sides. Add remaining ingredients. Simmer for 45 minutes or until chicken is tender. Serve over rice or pasta.

Chicken or Turkey Aspic

1 envelop UNFLAVORED GELATIN
¼ cup COLD WATER
½ cup HOT WATER
1 cup CHICKEN BROTH
2 Tbsp. LEMON JUICE
1 Tbsp. SHERRY
2 cups diced, cooked CHICKEN or TURKEY
½ cup thinly chopped CELERY
¼ cup thinly chopped ONION
¼ cup thinly chopped GREEN PEPPER

Soften gelatin in cold water. Add hot water. Cool to room temperature. Fold in chicken broth, lemon juice and sherry. Partially set. Fold in chicken or turkey, celery, onion and green pepper. Chill in salad bowl until firm.

Creekside Chicken or Turkey Salad

1/3 cup PLAIN YOGURT
¼ cup MAYONNAISE
½ tsp. LEMON JUICE
¼ cup DILL WEED
SALT and PEPPER to taste
1½ cups cubed, cooked CHICKEN or TURKEY
1/3 cup halved SPANISH OLIVES
1 small TOMATO, chopped
3 Tbsp. sliced GREEN ONION
AVOCADOES

In a large bowl mix together yogurt, mayonnaise, lemon juice, dill weed and seasoning. Stir in chicken or turkey, olives, tomato and green onions. Cover and chill thoroughly. Serve with sliced avocadoes placed around the bowl.

Stuffed Cornish Game Hens

A stuffed game hen is a meal in itself with rice and vegetables. Serve one per person with a salad for a delicious, festive meal.

1 GAME HEN per serving
1 6.2-oz. pkg. LONG GRAIN & WILD RICE
2 Tbsp. BUTTER
1 14-oz. can CHICKEN BROTH
1 4-oz. can MUSHROOMS
1 stalk CELERY, finely chopped
1 small ONION, chopped
1 firm APPLE, chopped
½ cup chopped WALNUT PIECES

Prepare game hens. Set aside. Cook the rice until slightly firm. In a bowl mix the rice with the remaining ingredients. Stuff the hens. Roast uncovered about an hour in a 350-degree oven or until done. Make a gravy from the drippings. Serve with the relish on page 22.

Turkey Tetrazzini

Submitted by Nancy Valenti, Lake Havasu City, Arizona

8 oz. SPAGHETTI
¼ cup BUTTER
¼ cup FLOUR
1 tsp. SALT
1/8 tsp. NUTMEG
2 cups canned CHICKEN BROTH
1 cup LIGHT CREAM
¼ cup MARSALA
¼ cup shredded PARMESAN CHEESE
½ cup cubed, cooked TURKEY
¼ cup chopped GREEN PEPPER
½ lb. MUSHROOMS, sliced
1 EGG YOLK
½ cup slivered ALMONDS

Break spaghetti in half. Boil for 3 minutes. Drain and put in a warm casserole dish. In a saucepan melt butter, blend in flour, salt, nutmeg. Stir constantly until smooth and bubbly. Remove from heat. Stir in broth and cream. Boil for 1 minute. Stir in wine and cheese. Add to the spaghetti. Mix in turkey, green pepper, mushrooms and egg yolk. Blend thoroughly. Sprinkle with slivered almonds. Bake in 350-degree oven for 25-30 minutes.

Cranberry-Pineapple Relish for Poultry

1 lb. bag CRANBERRIES
1 cup drained CRUSHED PINEAPPLE
½ cup crushed WALNUTS
2 cups SUGAR

Either grind the cranberries or cook them in water until they pop open. Cool. Add pineapple, walnuts and sugar. Let stand for several hours to blend flavors.

D is for Dutch Oven Cooking

Dutch Oven Glazed Ham

This recipe is a delicious way to cook ham in a Dutch oven.

1½ lbs. HAM SLICE
1 Tbsp. prepared MUSTARD
1 20-oz. can PEACHES or PINEAPPLE CHUNKS
½ cup packed BROWN SUGAR
WINE VINEGAR to taste
½ tsp. GROUND CLOVES

Place the ham slice in the bottom of the Dutch oven. Spread the mustard over the ham. Pour the fruit juice over the ham. Mix brown sugar and vinegar together. Spread over the ham. Add fruit. Sprinkle with cloves. Bury pot with coals and cook until ham is tender.

Vero Beach One-Pot Meal

1 lb. STEW MEAT, cut up into bite-size pieces
OIL
1 ONION, quartered
1 15-oz. can WHOLE WHITE POTATOES
4 CARROTS, thinly sliced
2 stalks CELERY, thinly sliced
¼ GREEN PEPPER, chopped into pieces
1 14.5-oz. can STEWED TOMATOES
1 14.5-oz. can PEAS or GREEN BEANS
2 Tbsp. FLOUR

In the Dutch oven brown the stew meat in oil. Add onion and cook until soft. Add remaining ingredients except flour. Cook with medium heat until all the vegetables are tender. Make a flour paste using the vegetable juice. Add to the stew. Cook until the stew has the desired thickness. Stew is better the second day!

Brown Rice and Chicken

White or yellow rice can be substituted.

1 cup BROWN RICE
1 4-lb. CHICKEN, cut up into pieces
1 dry ONION SOUP MIX
1 14.5-oz. can DICED TOMATOES
1 cup thinly sliced CELERY
1 14-oz. can CHICKEN BROTH
1 cup WATER
SALT and PEPPER to taste

Spread the rice at the bottom of the Dutch oven. Put the chicken pieces over the rice. Mix the onion soup with the tomatoes, celery and chicken broth. Add water. Pour over the chicken. Sprinkle seasoning over all. Cook 1 hour with coals on the top as well as underneath the pot.

Sweet and Sour Pork

1½ lbs. lean PORK CHOPS
1 medium ONION, sliced
SALT and PEPPER to taste
2 stalks CELERY, sliced
4 CARROTS, sliced
1 small GREEN PEPPER, chopped
1 4-oz. can MUSHROOMS
1 20-oz. can PINEAPPLE CHUNKS
¼ cup VINEGAR
2 Tbsp. SUGAR
1 Tbsp. CORNSTARCH
2 Tbsp. WATER

Brown meat in the Dutch oven with onions and seasoning. Add celery, carrots, green pepper, mushrooms and pineapple with the juice. Add vinegar and sugar. Cook until the meat and vegetables are done. Add cornstarch mixed with water. Cook until bubbly.

Spanish Rice

1 lb. GROUND BEEF
1 small ONION, chopped
1 stalk CELERY, thinly sliced
1/3 cup chopped GREEN PEPPER
1 14.5-oz. can DICED TOMATOES
1 14-oz. can BEEF BROTH
1 cup CHUNKY SALSA
GARLIC, SALT and PEPPER to taste
1 cup INSTANT RICE

Brown ground beef. Add onion, celery, and green pepper. Drain fat. Add tomatoes, beef broth and salsa. Season and simmer for 25 minutes. Add rice and cook until rice is done.

Goulash

2½ lbs. CHUCK STEAK, cut up in bite-size pieces
FLOUR
SALT and PEPPER to taste
1 tsp. GARLIC POWDER
2 tsp. PAPRIKA
VEGETABLE OIL
1 large ONION, chopped
1 clove GARLIC, crushed
1 14.5-oz. can ITALIAN STEWED TOMATOES
1 14-oz. can BEEF BROTH
1 16-oz. pkg. frozen PEAS and CARROTS
1 4-oz. can MUSHROOM PIECES
WIDE NOODLES, cooked and buttered

Roll beef in flour mixed with the seasoning. Brown in oil in a Dutch oven with onions and garlic. Pour off excess fat. Add tomatoes and beef broth. Simmer in a covered pot for 1 ½ hours, stirring occasionally. Add vegetables and mushrooms. Cook until meat is very tender. Serve with the cooked, buttered noodles.

Alamosa Chili Con Carne

1 lb. GROUND BEEF
1 large ONION, chopped
3 stalks CELERY, sliced
1 14.5-oz. can MEXICAN DICED TOMATOES
1 14.5-oz. can RED KIDNEY BEANS, undrained
1 Tbsp. CHILI POWDER
1 tsp. GARLIC POWDER

Brown the beef with the onions and celery in the Dutch oven. Pour off excess fat. Add remaining ingredients. Cook for 1½ to 2 hours.

Dutch Oven Baked Beans

½ lb. GROUND BEEF
1 small ONION, chopped
1 28-oz. can BAKED BEANS
1 tsp. MUSTARD
¼ cup BROWN SUGAR
¼ cup KETCHIP
SALT and PEPPER to taste
2 cups CRANBERRY JUICE

Brown the beef in the Dutch oven. Sauté onion until tender. Drain off excess fat. Pour off half of the juice from the beans. Add the beans with the rest of the remaining ingredients to the pot. Mix all together. Simmer for 1 hour. The tartness of the cranberries is a delicate change to the sweet beans.

*DUTCH OVEN IDEA: Use a round grill at the bottom of the Dutch oven to keep vegetables from sticking, or to warm up breads and biscuits.

E is for Eggs and Eggplant

Egg Nests

If you come back to camp tired after an active day, try this easy egg refresher. I like French or sourdough bread rather than plain white or wheat but it is a matter of preference.

BUTTER
1 slice of FRENCH or SOURDOUGH BREAD per serving
1 EGG for each
FAVORITE CHEESE
SALT and PEPPER to taste

At the bottom of a skillet melt the butter. Do not use a high heat.

Hollow out the center of the bread. Lay it in the buttered skillet. Lightly toast and turn. Drop an egg in the center hollow. Season with salt and pepper. Cover with cheese. Cover the skillet and cook until the egg is done.

Mushroom and Tomato Omelet

1 14.5-oz. can ITALIAN DICED TOMATOES
1 4-oz. can MUSHROOM PIECES
2 Tbsp. chopped ONION
1 tsp. SUGAR
CELERY SALT and PEPPER to taste
6 EGGS
½ cup MILK
BUTTER
½ cup shredded MONTEREY JACK CHEESE

In a saucepan combine tomatoes, mushrooms, onions and seasonings. Simmer gently for 5 minutes on low heat. Set aside. Beat the eggs and milk together. Melt the butter in a skillet. Pour in egg mixture. Stir constantly while cooking the eggs. When done, place on a platter. Pour half of the sauce and half the cheese over the eggs. Fold over. Pour remaining sauce and cheese on the side.

Breakfast Eggs with Potatoes

1 Tbsp. BUTTER
1 14.5-oz. can SLICED POTATOES
½ lb. sliced MOZZARELLA CHEESE
6 to 8 EGGS
SALT and PEPPER to taste
3 Tbsp. grated PARMESAN CHEESE
1 Tbsp. BUTTER

Melt the butter in a skillet. Arrange the potatoes at the bottom of the pan. With low heat gently simmer to warm. Cover with mozzarella cheese. Break the eggs over the cheese. In a cup, mix the seasoning and parmesan cheese together. Sprinkle over the eggs. Dot with butter. Simmer over low heat until the eggs are done and the cheese is melted.

For variety, replace the butter with olive oil and fry the potatoes.

Scrambled Eggs with Salsa

4 slices BACON
1/2 cup chopped GREEN PEPPER
1/3 cup chopped ONIONS
8 EGGS, beaten
1 cup small curd COTTAGE CHEESE
½ cup MONTEREY JACK CHEESE
½ cup SALSA

In a skillet cook the bacon slices. Crumble the bacon. Set aside. In the skillet cook the green pepper and onions until tender. In a bowl mix the eggs with the cottage cheese. Add the crumbled bacon and vegetables to the egg and cheese. Place the egg mixture in the skillet. Cook and gently stir 2 to 4 minutes. Add jack cheese and salsa. Cook until eggs are set.

Scrambled Eggs with Asparagus

The green asparagus is a lovely compliment to the yellow eggs.

10 EGGS
1 cup MILK
SALT and PEPPER to taste
½ of 4-oz. can MUSHROOM PIECES
2 Tbsp. BUTTER or MARGARINE
1 cup shredded, favorite CHEESE
Fresh ASPARAGUS SPEARS, cooked
PAPRIKA and PARSLEY FLAKES

Whisk the eggs and milk together in a bowl. Add seasoning and mushrooms. In a skillet melt the butter. Add the egg mixture with the cheese. Cook over low heat, stirring constantly until the eggs are done. Place on a serving platter. Top with asparagus spears. Sprinkle paprika and parsley on top for added color.

Egg Loaf Salad

6 HARD-COOKED EGGS, chopped
¼ cup chopped SPANISH OLIVES
¼ cup SWEET RELISH
1 tsp MINCED ONION
1 tsp. chopped GREEN PEPPER
½ tsp. MUSTARD
SALT and PEPPER to taste
PARSLEY
3 Tbsp. MAYONNAISE

Mix all ingredients until well blended. Press the mixture into a waxed paper or foil-covered loaf pan or bowl. Chill several hours or overnight. Serve as a salad with lettuce, cut up tomatoes and cucumbers. Or, slice and use as a base for a delicious sandwich.

Eggplant Fritters

1 large EGGPLANT
¼ cup SALTED WATER
1 EGG, beaten
1 medium ONION, minced
SALT and PEPPER to taste
1/3 cup FLOUR
1 tsp. BAKING POWDER
2 Tbsp. TOMATO SAUCE.
HOT OIL

Peel and cube eggplant. Place in water and cook until tender. Drain, mash and cool. Stir in egg, onions and seasoning. In a cup mix flour and baking powder together. Stir into the eggplant. Add enough tomato sauce to make a batter. Drop by spoonful into the hot oil. Cook both sides until brown.

Eggplant Deluxe

1 medium EGGPLANT
½ cup ITALIAN SALAD DRESSING
¾ cup HERBED BREAD CRUMBS
6 CHICKEN THIGHS, discard skin
SALT and PEPPER to taste
1 16-oz. jar MEATLESS SPAGHETTI SAUCE
6 thick slabs MOZZARELLA CHEESE

Peel the eggplant. Cut into 6 slices. Brush each side with salad dressing. Dip each side of the slices into the bread crumbs.

Place on a cookie sheet. Brush each side of chicken thighs with salad dressing and bread crumbs. Place on the cookie sheet alongside the eggplant. Sprinkle seasoning over all. Bake in a 400-degree oven for 30 minutes. Place each thigh on top of eggplant. Spread the sauce on top. Cover with cheese. Bake 10 minutes more or until sauce is bubbly and the cheese is melted.

Eggplant Salad

1 large EGGPLANT, peeled and cubed
WATER
2 HARD-COOKED EGGS, chopped
1 Tbsp. chopped RED ONION
1 Tbsp. chopped DILL PICKLE
1 tsp. LEMON JUICE
2 Tbsp. MAYONNAISE

Cook the eggplant in water until tender. Mash. Add chopped eggs, and remaining ingredients. Chill thoroughly. Serve on a bed of lettuce with sliced tomatoes on the side.

North Fork Eggplant Patties

2 small EGGPLANT
1 small ONION, finely minced
½ GREEN PEPPER, chopped
1 tsp. CELERY SALT
1 Tbsp. chopped PARSLEY
1 EGG, well beaten
½ cup ITALIAN BREAD CRUMBS
Hot OLIVE OIL

Peel off the skin. Cube and cook the eggplant until tender. Mash. Add remaining ingredients except the oil. Mix well. Form into patties. Fry patties in hot oil, browning on both sides.

Eggplant a la Mikesell

Submitted by Marjorie Mikesell, Eugene, Oregon

"Sometimes I add shrimp or leftover meat to this recipe."

In a skillet cook a cubed EGGPLANT in olive oil. Add chopped RED ONION, CELERY and GREEN PEPPER. Sauté until tender. Add a can of DICED TOMATOES. Season with PARSLEY, SALT and PEPPER to taste. Cover and simmer until done.

F is for Fish

Pineapple and Bass

1½ lbs. BASS FILLETS
1 20-oz. can PINEAPPLE CHUNKS
1 Tbsp. LEMON or LIME JUICE
1 Tbsp. WORCESTERSHIRE SAUCE
SALT and PEPPER to taste

Place the fillets in a shallow baking pan. Combine the juice of the pineapple with the other liquids and seasoning. Pour over the fillets. Marinate for 1 hour at least, turning once. Drain and reserve the marinade to baste the fish while cooking. Grill the fish until done. Serve with pineapple chunks.

Havasu Fried Bass

1½ cups CORN FLAKES, crushed
½ tsp. ITALIAN DRESSING
¼ tsp. GARLIC SALT
1 EGG, beaten
BASS FILLETS
Hot OIL

In a bowl combine corn flakes crumbs, Italian seasoning and garlic salt. Prepare fillets, if necessary. Dip the fillets in the beaten egg, then in the crumb mixture. Fry in the hot oil until brown on both sides and flaky. If you have an oven, bake at 350-degree until done.

This is a good way to cook yellowtail or trout.

Whole Fried Fish

If you have small fish, fry them in PANCAKE FLOUR combined with ONION POWDER. Moisten with BEER or CLUB SODA to make a thick and creamy batter. Fry in a well-oiled skillet until fish is brown and flaky.

Oceanside Fish Burgers

1 lb. cooked, flaked FISH
1 EGG, slightly beaten
1 tsp. LEMON JUICE
½ cup HERBED BREAD CRUMBS
1 small ONION, chopped
1 Tbsp. chopped PARSLEY
½ cup MAYONNAISE
½ tsp. ROSEMARY
Dash of PEPPER
2 Tbsp. grated PARMESAN CHEESE, optional

Combine all ingredients in a bowl. Mix well. Form into 4 patties. Fry in a skillet with hot oil or cook on the grill, browning on both sides. Serve with hamburger buns, pickles and lettuce.

Cornbread Crusted Fish Fillets

1 EGG
½ cup CORNMEAL MUFFIN MIX
1 tsp. CHILI POWDER
¼ tsp. CAYENNE POWDER
SALT and PEPPER to taste
VEGETABLE OIL
Fish Fillets

Beat the egg in a bowl. In another larger bowl combine the cornmeal mix with the seasonings. If you are frying, use vegetable oil. If grilling, brown on both sides. Serve with tartar sauce.

Tartar Sauce

Combine 1 Tbsp. of SWEET PICKLE RELISH with ½ Tbsp. minced ONION, 1 Tbsp. chopped PARSLEY, 1 Tbsp. finely chopped SPANISH OLIVES and 2 Tbsp. MAYONNAISE.

Oh! Ridge Fish Fritters

1½ lb. cooked, firm FISH
3 EGGS, separated
3 Tbsp. FLOUR
1 Tbsp. chopped PARSLEY
¼ tsp. GARLIC POWDER
½ tsp. ONION POWDER
¼ tsp. PAPRIKA
½ tsp. THYME
SALT and PEPPER to taste

Mash the fish in a bowl. Beat the egg yolks until light. Beat egg whites at room temperature until foamy. Add the remaining ingredients into the egg yolks. Fold egg whites into the mixture. Heat oil. Drop the batter into the hot oil by spoonful. Fry until golden brown on both sides. Serve with tartar sauce.

Twin Lakes Fish Pie

If you have more fish than you can use at one time, cook the fish and save it for this fish pie another day.

2 Tbsp. BUTTER
2 Tbsp. FLOUR
SALT and PEPPER to taste
1 cup MILK
2 cups cooked, flaked FISH
¾ cup cooked PEAS
1 Tbsp. chopped ONION
1 Tbsp chopped CELERY
1 Tbsp. chopped GREEN PEPPER
1 cup MASHED POTATOES

Melt butter in a saucepan. Add flour and seasoning. Add milk. Beat until creamy. Add fish, peas, onion, celery and green pepper. Pour into buttered casserole dish. Top with mashed potatoes. Bake in a 375-degree oven for 12-15 minutes.

Stanley Basin Trout Salad

2 cups cooked TROUT
1 cup chopped CELERY
¼ cup SWEET PICKLE RELISH
SALT and PEPPER to taste
¼ tsp. ONION POWDER
MAYONNAISE
1 HARD-COOKED EGG, sliced
PAPRIKA

Flake the fish. Be sure there are no bones. Add celery, relish and seasonings. Moisten with mayonnaise. Serve on salad greens with the sliced egg and paprika sprinkled on top.

Trout Fried with Oatmeal

1 large, or a small trout for each serving
1 EGG, beaten
1 cup quick-cooking OATMEAL
SALT and PEPPER to taste
2 Tbsp. OLIVE OIL
LEMON WEDGES

Dip the trout in the egg. Combine the oatmeal with the seasoning. Dip the trout in the oatmeal. Heat the oil in the skillet and fry on both sides until done. Garnish with lemon wedges.

Tuna-Cheese Sandwiches

Drain a 6-oz. can of TUNA and place in a bowl. Add a chopped HARD-COOKED EGG, chopped ONION and SWEET PICKLE RELISH. Add just a squirt of LEMON JUICE. Moisten with MAYONNAISE. Add SALT and PEPPER to taste. Toast two slices of bread per serving. Spread the tuna mixture and a slice of SWISS CHEESE on the toast. Serve with a dill pickle.

Sauteed Salmon Steaks

2 SALMON STEAKS
SALT and PEPPER to taste
FLOUR
2 Tbsp. VEGETABLE OIL
2 cups cooked, chopped SPINACH
1 clove GARLIC, minced
1 Tbsp. LEMON JUICE
1 tsp. chopped THYME
2 MUSHROOMS, sliced

Season the steaks. Dust with flour. In hot oil sauté the steaks, turning once, until done. Arrange the cooked spinach on a heated platter. Lay the salmon on top. Keep warm. Sauté the garlic, lemon juice, thyme and mushrooms. Cook until the mushrooms are done. Pour over the steaks.

Ketchican Salmon and Potato Dish

1 14.5 oz. can WHOLE WHITE POTATOES
1 medium ONION, chopped
½ cup sliced MUSHROOMS
SALT and PEPPER to taste
¼ tsp. GARLIC POWDER
1 Tbsp. chopped PARSLEY
¼ cup OLIVE OIL
4 SALMON STEAKS

Butter a baking dish. Spread half of the potatoes at the bottom of the dish. Over the potatoes spread half of the onions, mushrooms, seasonings and oil. Place salmon steaks on top. Spread the remaining potatoes, onions, mushrooms, seasoning and oil over the steaks. Bake in a 400-degree oven for 30-35 minutes or until steaks are done.

G is for GRILLING

Grilling Ideas

1. Grill extra steak, chicken, pork or ham to use for sandwiches, leftover dishes or salads.

2. Keep flour tortillas on hand to use as wrappers for meat, grilled vegetables, egg dishes or fish.

3. Plan to make the marinade ahead at night to use the next day for the dinner meat or fish. Store in the refrigerator.

4. Check recipes for the food of the day to be sure the ingredients are at hand or can be purchased during the day.

5. Use a long-handled tong instead of a fork when grilling for an easy turn-over of foods and foiled packages.

6. Use basting brushes of various sizes for sauces and marinades. Have on hand long metal kabobs to use for meats and vegetables. If using bamboo kabobs, soak in water first.

7. Have two grill racks, one for meats and one for fish.

8. A good marinade for fish or chicken is a mixture of FRESH HERBS, GARLIC, OLIVE OIL and LEMON JUICE.

Grilled Bread

Everyone loves grilled bread with grilled food.

Halve the FRENCH or ITALIAN loaf horizontally. Brush sides with OLIVE OIL or BUTTER mixed with PARMESAN CHEESE and MINCED PARSLEY. Place over hot coals for about 3 minutes on each side depending on the heat of the fire.

A Good Marinade for Grilling Beef and Pork

1/3 cup OLIVE OIL
1/3 cup RED WINE VINEGAR
3 Tbsp. SOY SAUCE
1 Tbsp. ONION POWDER
1 clove GARLIC, minced
½ tsp. MINCED PARSLEY
Coarse GROUND PEPPER and SALT to taste

Mix all ingredients together and keep in a jar in the refrigerator. Double the recipe to keep on hand to use for more than one meal.

Portion out what you need for the first day and discard any marinade that you use or have leftover that day. Keep the remainder in the jar in the refrigerator.

Eastport Grilled Eggplant

Grill the EGGPLANT whole in its skin until it blisters, blackens and becomes limp. Carefully scoop out the pulp. Mash with a fork. In a cup mix a tsp. each of LEMON JUICE, OLIVE OIL and GARLIC. Mix with the eggplant pulp and serve. This is a good side dish with grilled chicken or beef. Sliced tomatoes and cucumbers goes well with this dish also.

Boise Grilled Potatoes

5 medium Idaho BAKING POTATOES
1 medium ONION, sliced
MARGARINE
1/3 cup shredded CHEDDAR CHEESE
1 Tbsp. WORCESTERSHIRE SAUCE
SALT and PEPPER to taste
PARSLEY
7-oz.of BROTH - CHICKEN or BEEF

Peel and cube the potatoes. Put the potatoes and onions in the middle of a large piece of heavy-duty foil. Dot with margarine. Combine the cheese with Worcestershire sauce and seasonings. Sprinkle over the potatoes. Add the broth. Carefully fold up and secure to prevent leakage. Grill over medium coals for 35 minutes or until potatoes are tender.

Grilled Green Pepper

Foil wrap whole peppers. Place over direct heat for 15 minutes or until blackened. Carefully unwrap and serve.

Grilled Sweet Potatoes

Wrap in foil. Cook for 1½ hours over medium direct heat.

Grilled Mushrooms

If using bamboo kabob skewers soak in water for 30 minutes. In the meantime clean the MUSHROOMS with a damp paper towel. When skewers are ready thread the mushrooms on them. Brush with OLIVE OIL and SALT and PEPPER, to taste. Grill 7 to 10 minutes, turning occasionally. For an added attraction, between each mushroom place pieces of GREEN PEPPER and whole CHERRY TOMATOES.

Topeka Stuffed Tomatoes

4 large, firm TOMATOES
½ cup HERBED BREAD CRUMBS
1 Tbsp. PARMESAN CHEESE
1 6-oz. can TUNA, drained
½ tsp. SWEET PICKLE RELISH
¼ cup chopped ONION
¼ cup chopped CELERY
½ cup shredded MOZZARELLA CHEESE
Melted BUTTER to moisten

Scoop out center of tomato leaving a shell. Cut up center pulp and mix with remaining ingredients. Mix well. Stuff each tomato shell. Wrap each shell in foil. Grill for 30 minutes or until tomatoes are tender.

Fresh Tomato Grilled with Mozzarella

1 lb. Large-size ROMA TOMATOES
1 lb. MOZZARELLA, cut into ¼" slices
SPINACH and LETTUCE LEAVES
¼ tsp. Dijon-style MUSTARD
1 Tbsp. RED WINE VINEGAR
Pinch of SUGAR, SALT and PEPPER

Cut tomatoes, lengthwise, into ¼" pieces. Grill on the barbecue both sides until brown. When done, alternately place mozzarella with tomatoes on a plate of spinach and lettuce leaves. Mix mustard, vinegar, seasonings. Spread over the top and grill.

Yakama Grilled Granny Smith Apples

4 Granny Smith APPLES, unpeeled
¼ cup, packed BROWN SUGAR
¼ tsp. LEMON ZEST
½ cup RAISINS
1 tsp. CINNAMON

Core apples. Mix together brown sugar, lemon zest and raisins. Fill the apple centers with mixture. Sprinkle cinnamon on top. Place apples on a pie plate, or equivalent. Wrap the apples in foil and place on grill. Cook for 15 minutes.

Kansas Grilled Corn-on-the-Cob

CORN-on-the-COB, one each serving, unhusked
Cold, salted WATER
½ cup softened BUTTER
SALT and PEPPER to taste

Soak corn in the water for 2 hours. When ready, place over hot coals on the grill and roast until the husks are brown, at least 10 minutes. Unwrap. Butter and season. Wrap in foil and grill.

Best Ever Grilled Trout

Submitted by Betty Hommerding, Escondido, California

Spread Best Foods MAYONNAISE inside and out of trout. If small to medium, one trout to a serving. Do not substitute the mayonnaise. Spray the barbecue grill with a non-stick cooking spray. Grill the fish for 15 minutes on each side, turning once. Large fish may take a bit longer. There is something about the mayonnaise that makes this superb.

Grilled Salmon Kabobs

1 lb. SALMON, cut up into bite-size pieces
¼ cup OLIVE OIL
¼ cup chopped ONION
¼ tsp. each ROSEMARY and THYME
1/3 cup ORANGE JUICE
1 tsp. ORANGE ZEST
12 fresh MUSHROOMS, cut in half if large
12 ORANGE WEDGES
12 CUCUMBER CHUNKS

Marinate the salmon with a mixture of oil, onions, seasonings, orange juice and orange zest at least for 1 hour. Thread the salmon, mushrooms, orange wedges and cucumber chunks on 4 skewers. Place on a non-stick cooking sprayed grill. Turn and brush with the marinade several times. Grill for 8-10 minutes or until the fish flakes.

Grilled Meat Basil Butter Sauce

In a saucepan stir 2 Tbsp. finely chopped FRESH BASIL and 1 tsp. LEMON JUICE with ½ cup softened unsalted BUTTER. Spoon into a covered container. Keep in refrigerator until ready to use. Spread over grilled meat and vegetables for that special touch.

Grilled Sausages

KIELBASA, SWEET ITALIAN, BRATWURST and SAUSAGES are especially tasty when barbecued on the grill. Spray the grill with non-stick cooking spray to prevent the sausages from sticking while cooking. Place on the grill. Turn several times to cook evenly. Use tongs, not a fork to turn them. If the skin is punctured, the juices will flow out.

Wipperts Grilled Cheeseburgers

½ lb. SWEET ITALIAN SAUSAGES, casing removed
2 lbs. GROUND BEEF
½ cup BREAD CRUMBS
2 Tbsp. chopped ONION
½ cup KETCHUP
2 Tbsp. PARMESAN CHEESE
SALT and PEPPER to taste
4 slices SHARP CHEDDAR CHEESE

Combine all ingredients in a bowl except cheddar cheese. Mix together with your hands. Shape into 4 patties. Grill over coals until done. Remove from heat. Keep warm. Toast the buns on the grill. Assemble the burger on the bun topped with cheese.

Grilled Pork Chops

Using the marinade of your choice, marinate the pork chops for 3 to 4 hours, reserving about 1 cup for basting. Grill over hot coals about 7 minutes each side, until brown. Turn with tongs so as not to puncture the meat. Brush with the reserved marinade each time.

It is a good time to try the grilled apples on page 40, to enjoy with the pork. Applesauce is also tasty with pork chops. Spice up with a can of applesauce adding cinnamon, cloves or nuts and raisins.

Coos Bay Trout with Mushroom Sauce

4 TROUT FILLETS
1 10.5-oz can CREAM of MUSHROOM SOUP
2 tsp. WORCESTERSHIRE SAUCE
¼ tsp. THYME
PARSLEY
1/8 cup LEMON JUICE
LEMON WEDGES

Make four aluminum foil squares. Place a fillet on each. Mix the soup, Worcestershire sauce and thyme together. Pour over fillets. Sprinkle parsley and lemon juice over fish. Wrap up and secure foil squares. Place over medium-hot coals. Grill until done.

Sedona Grilled London Broil

1/3 cup OLIVE OIL
1/3 cup RED WINE VINEGAR
3 Tbsp. SOY SAUCE
GARLIC POWDER
½ tsp. coarse GROUND PEPPER
FLANK STEAK
2 medium ONIONS, sliced OR
1 RED ONION, sliced

Mix marinade. Pour over beef. Cover and refrigerate 3 to 4 hours, turning each hour. Remove meat. Reserve marinade. Grill with hot coals for 5 to 6 minutes on each side, depending on the thickness of the steak. Brush with the marinade on each side several times. Place onions on grill until lightly brown. When serving the London broil, cut diagonally across the grain into thin slices. Serve with the onions. Sourdough rolls and a green salad goes well with the steak.

A simple marinade of 1 Tbsp. SOY SAUCE mixed with 2 Tbsp. OLIVE OIL is also good. Grill 6 minutes each side.

H is for Holiday Ideas

Bloody Mary Aspic

This is a refreshing lunch idea to welcome the New Year.

2 envelopes UNFLAVORED GELATIN
2 cups BLOODY MARY MIX
1 BAY LEAF
1 ½ cups WATER
½ tsp. SALT
¼ tsp. SUGAR
LETTUCE
COTTAGE CHEESE with CHIVES
Large cooked SHRIMP

In a medium saucepan sprinkle the gelatin over the Bloody Mary mix. Add the bay leaf. Cook over low heat, stirring constantly until the gelatin is dissolved. Remove from heat. Remove bay leaf. Stir in water and seasonings. Pour into a ring mold. Chill until firm. Unmold on a bed of lettuce. Place cottage cheese in the center of the mold. Top with shrimp. Serve with mayonnaise on the side.

Cocoa Eggnog

For a chocoholic, this a good way to start the New Year.

1 EGG WHITE
1 tsp. SUGAR
1 tsp. COCOA
SALT
¼ cup cold MILK
½ tsp. VANILLA

Beat the egg white until stiff. In a bowl sift together sugar, cocoa and salt. Slowly add to the egg white. Fold in milk and vanilla. Gently mix all together. Measurements are per serving.

Strawberry Gelatin with Strawberries

This is a suggestion to serve for Valentine's Day

1 pkg. STRAWBERRY-FLAVORED GELATIN
1 cup BOILING WATER
1 cup COLD WATER
Fresh STRAWBERRIES, rinsed and hulled

Follow the directions on the package to make the gelatin. If the strawberries are large cut in half before adding to the gelatin mixture. Serve with whipped cream.

Lime Yuck

For St. Patrick's Day try this delicious green side-dish.

1 large pkg. LIME-FLAVORED GELATIN
1 20-oz. can CRUSHED PINEAPPLE, drained
1 16-oz.container COTTAGE CHEESE
½ cup chopped WALNUT
1 10-oz. can CHUNKY MIXED FRUIT
12 small-size MARSHMELLOWS

Make the gelatin according to directions on the package. Omit ½ cup of water. Partially set. Fold in the rest of the ingredients. Mix well. Pour into a bowl. Chill. It can be served in the bowl or on a bed of lettuce.

Wausau Baked Corned Beef

Instead of boiling the corned beef for St. Patrick's Day dinner, bake it. Place the fat side up of a CORNED BEEF roast in a baking dish. Cover with foil. Bake in a 350-degree oven for 2½ hours or until the roast is tender. In a small bowl mix 1 tsp. MUSTARD and ½ cup BROWN SUGAR together. Score the roast. Spread the brown sugar mixture on top. Continue to bake the roast for another 5 minutes. Cool about 15 to 20 minutes before slicing.

Virginia Ham Steaks

This is an easy oven dish if you are having ham for Easter when camping.

1½" slice of HAM STEAK
1 14.5-oz. can DICED TOMATOES
½ of 4-oz. can MUSHROOMS
¼ cup PARMESAN CHEESE

Place the ham in a baking dish. Spread the tomatoes and mushrooms over it. Cover and bake in a 350-degree oven for 30 minutes. Uncover. Sprinkle the cheese over the ham. Bake for 15 minutes more or until done.

Ham and Cabbage Mold

1 Tbsp. UNFLAVORED GELATIN
¼ cup COLD WATER
1¼ cups HOT WATER
1 Tbsp. VINEGAR
SALT to taste
¾ cup MAYONNAISE
1 tsp. MUSTARD
1½ cups cooked HAM, cut up into bite-size pieces
1 cup shredded CABBAGE
2 Tbsp. minced ONION
2 Tbsp. chopped GREEN PEPPER

Soften gelatin in cold water. Add hot water. Stir to dissolve the gelatin. Add vinegar and salt. Cool to room temperature. Stir in mayonnaise and mustard. Partially set. Add ham, cabbage, onion and green pepper. Pour into a mold and chill until firm.

Ideas for Hard-Cooked Easter Eggs

Mix the yolks with mayonnaise and CHUTNEY, CAVIER, FOIS GRAS, CHOPPED CHIVES or CAPERS and stuff the shells.

Fourth-of-July Fruit Cup

HONEYDEW MELON, cut up into bite-size pieces
STRAWBERRIES, rinsed and hulled
Fresh BLUEBERRIES
½ to1Tbsp. SUGAR, optional

In a bowl combine the fruit with the sugar, depending on personal taste. Chill before serving in individual fruit cups. Top with whipped cream for a festive touch.

Yankee Doodle Salad

This is an easy picnic salad for the Fourth of July

2 cups cooked MACARONI
1 12-oz. can LUNCHEON MEAT, cubed
½ cup grated PARMESAN CHEESE
½ cup chopped CUCUMBER
¼ cup chopped RED ONION
1 tsp. SALT
½ cup SALAD DRESSING
PARMESAN CHEESE, optional

Combine all the ingredients except the salad dressing. Toss well. Mix the salad dressing with the salad. Chill. Before serving, add more salad dressing if needed. Sprinkle the parmesan cheese on top for an added touch. If you have leftover beef, pork or chicken cut up into bite-size pieces and substitute for the luncheon meat.

To go with this salad, marinate with ITALIAN DRESSING, sliced CUCUMBER, sliced TOMATOES, sliced RED ONION and sliced GREEN and/or RED PEPPER. Make in layers in a quart jar or sealed container. Chill before serving. Make more than for a single meal quantity. Keep the vegetables with the Italian dressing in the container in the refrigerator. It will stay fresh for some time. Use with a bed of lettuce for an easy salad.

Dilly Beans

Submitted by Sue Clagg, Arroyo Grande, California

"These beans are a delicious picnic and colorful side dish when home-grown green beans are picked or are fresh in the market."

½ of 14-oz. can BEEF BROTH
2 Tbsp. chopped ONION
½ cup chopped GREEN PEPPER
½ tsp. DILL WEED
1 lb. fresh whole GREEN BEANS

Cook the broth, onion, green pepper and dill weed for several minutes to blend flavors. Prepare the beans and add to the broth. Cook the beans until tender about 6-8 minutes.

"If you like Dilly Beans, can them when they are fresh in the market or fresh from the garden. It is not hard to do" —Sue Clagg.

3 lbs. young GREEN BEANS, cut off ends
½ cup of fresh DILL
2 cloves GARLIC
DILL SPRIGS
GARLIC PIECES
2 cups WATER
2 cups VINEGAR
4 Tbsp. SALT
5 Tbsp. SUGAR
½ tsp. CAYENNE PEPPER

Boil prepared beans with dill and garlic. Leave beans whole. When tender, pack into sterilized pint jars standing up. Add dill sprigs and garlic among the beans. Heat to boiling the water, vinegar, salt, sugar and cayenne pepper. Pour into the jars with beans and seal with canning lids.

Heavenly Hash

'This is a good recipe for Hot August Nights as it is refreshing, cool looking and taste great." —Neva Kelsey, Redding, California

1 20-oz. can PINEAPPLE CHUNKS
1 20-oz. can PEAR HALVES, quartered
1 large jar CHERRIES, diced
1 pkg. large MARSHMALLOWS, quartered (use scissors)
1 pint SOUR CREAM

Drain all the fruit in a sieve. Mix the fruit in a large bowl with the marshmallows. Fold in the sour cream. Cover and chill.

Along with the fruit, serve a special GRILLED ASPARAGUS for a cool, attractive dish.

1 lb. fresh ASPARAGUS
4 Tbsp. extra virgin OLIVE OIL
SALT and PEPPER to taste

Bend to break off the bottom of the asparagus or cut off the bottom white portion that is tough. Place in a plate and cover the asparagus spears with oil. Cook on a medium-hot grill. Turn and roll the spears until brown, but not burnt.

Halloween-Glazed Carrots

1 lb. bag fresh BABY CARROTS, sliced into sticks
1 cup boiled, salted WATER
½ tsp. ORANGE ZEST
1 whole ORANGE, cut up in segments
2 Tbsp. BUTTER or MARGARINE
3 Tbsp. MAPLE SYRUP

Boil carrots in water until tender. Add orange zest and oranges, butter and syrup. Cook over low heat until butter is melted and oranges are heated.

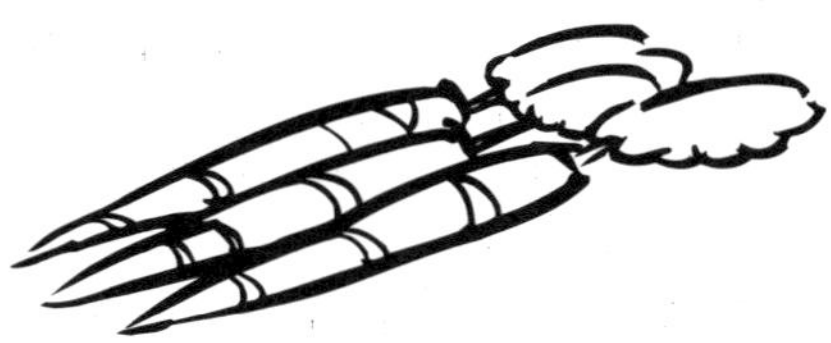

Pumpkin Casserole

What to do with the pumpkin pulp leftover from the jack-o-lantern? Try this easy side dish with ham.

3 or 4 cups chopped PUMPKIN, no seeds or stringy parts
¼ cup melted BUTTER
¼ cup MILK
3 EGGS, well beaten
2 Tbsp. BREAD CRUMBS
1 Tbsp. finely chopped ONION
SALT and PEPPER to taste

In a saucepan cover the pumpkin with water. Cook until tender. Mash. Drain. Add remaining ingredients. Place in a casserole dish. Bake in a 350-degree oven for 45 minutes.

Sweet Potato—Sausage Dressing

This is a different, delicious dressing, enough for a roasting chicken or a small Thanksgiving turkey. Rye bread adds a unique flavor, but white or sourdough bread is fine.

6 slices RYE BREAD, toasted and cubed
1 cup mashed SWEET POTATOES
½ cup chopped CELERY
½ lb. PORK SAUSAGE
3 Tbsp. minced ONION
SALT and PEPPER to taste
1 tsp. POULTRY SEASONING

Combine bread cubes, sweet potato and celery. In a skillet cook the sausage until done. Crumble. Add to the bread and potato mixture. Sauté the onions in the sausage fat until tender. Add to the dressing mixture. Season to taste. Mix together until well blended. Stuff the bird or bake the dressing in the oven separately. If I bake it in the oven, sometimes I spread parmesan cheese on top before baking as an added flavor.

Thanksgiving Salad

1 15.4-oz. can PINEPPLE CHUNKS
1 6-oz. pkg. ORANGE-FLAVORED GELATIN
1 cup COLD WATER
1 16-oz. can WHOLE CRANBERRY SAUCE
1 cup chopped CELERY
½ cup chopped DATES
½ cup chopped WALNUTS

Drain the pineapple chunks, reserving the juice. To the pineapple juice add enough water to make a cup of liquid. Bring the juice to a boil. Add orange gelatin. Stir until dissolved. Add the cold water and mix in. Chill until partially set. Fold in the remaining ingredients. Pour into a fancy mold. Chill until firm.

Apple—Raisin—Walnut Stuffing

Try something different for the Thanksgiving turkey.
It is so crunchy and delicious.

1 box STUFFING MIX
½ cup chopped ONIONS
½ cup chopped CELERY
1 cup chopped raw APPLE
½ cup seedless RAISINS
½ cup chopped WALNUTS
CRANBERRY JUICE

Follow the directions on the stuffing package to make the basic stuffing. Mix in the apple, raisins and walnuts. Add enough cranberry juice to moisten.

FYI - If you have a large pot, with CHICKEN BROTH and water cover the TURKEY BONES. Simmer with ONIONS, PEAS, CELERY, CARROTS for a delicious soup. Put in excess dressing and gravy. Season to taste with salt, pepper and poultry seasoning.

Christmas Rice

1½ cups INSTANT RICE
1 Tbsp. MARGARINE
1 14-oz. can CHICKEN BROTH
¼ cup chopped fresh PARSLEY
½ cup chopped GREEN PEPPER
½ cup thinly sliced CELERY
1 14.5-oz.can DICED TOMATOES

In a saucepan combine rice, margarine and chicken broth. Cook until rice is done. Add remaining ingredients. Simmer for 8 to 10 minutes more to blend all flavors.

Christmas Pie

Submitted by Wendy Sara-May Miller, Peoria, Arizona

1 10-oz. pkg. frozen SPINACH
1 16-oz. container COTTAGE CHEESE
4 EGGS, beaten
1 cup shredded MOZZARELLA CHEESE
1/3 cup grated PARMESAN CHEESE
½ cup chopped RED PEPPER
1 tsp. ITALIAN SEASONINGS

Thaw, drain and chop spinach. In a large bowl mix spinach with the remaining ingredients. Pour into a greased 9" pie plate. Bake in a 350-degree oven for 40-45 minutes or until the center is set.

Elves Cheese and Whiskey Spread

½ lb. ROQUEFORT CHEESE
½ lb. CREAM CHEESE
½ cup WHISKEY

Mix the cheeses together. Add the whiskey to bind the cheeses. Place in a covered container. Keep in the refrigerator.

Noel Pudding

Submitted by Heather Fanshawe, Queensland, Australia

2 cups FLOUR
2 cups minced DRIED FRUIT
1 cup SUGAR
½ Tbsp. BAKING SODA
½ tsp. MIXED SPICES (cloves, ginger, allspice or nutmeg)
2 cups MILK
2 Tbsp. BUTTER
RUM, optional

In a saucepan boil together milk and butter. Cool. In a large bowl mix the dry ingredients together. Mix in the rum. Add the milk mixture. Fill 10 greased oven proof ramekins or cups with mixture or fill a pudding bowl. Cook ramekins in slow oven or boil if using a pudding bowl.

Christmas Party Snack

"These are a great hit at our family parties at Christmas Eve."

—Eloise Knowland, Seattle, Washington

1 RED BELL PEPPER, quartered into wedges
2 GREEN BELL PEPPERS, quartered into wedges
¾ cup CREAM CHEESE with CHIVES, softened
1½ Tbsp. chopped SPANISH OLIVES
4 Tbsp. shredded MONTEREY JACK CHEESE or
shredded COLBY CHEESE
PAPRIKA

Prepare the peppers and place on a baking sheet. Mix the cream cheese and chopped olives together. Divide the mixture into the twelve wedges. Cover with the shredded cheese. Sprinkle paprika on top. Place on the grill with medium heat and cook for 10 - 15 minutes or until the bottom of the peppers begin to blister. These wedges can also be baked in a medium oven.

is for International Cooking

Irish Coffee

It is a breach of etiquette to mix the coffee. Drink it through the whipped cream. Ingredients are per serving.

2 tsp. SUGAR
2/3 cup HOT BLACK COFFEE
2 Tbsp. IRISH WHISKEY
Spoonful of WHIPPED CREAM

Rinse a large wine glass with warm water. Add the sugar. Fill the glass 2/3 full of hot coffee. stir gently. Add the whiskey. Top with whipped cream. Enjoy.

Irish Whiskey Highball

Place 2 ice cubes in a highball glass. Add 1 jigger per serving of IRISH WHISKEY, ¼ tsp. LEMON ZEST. Fill the glass with GINGER ALE.

Irish Potato Scrapple

This is an answer to potato chips!

1 cup cold MASHED POTATOES
1 cup cooked shredded CABBAGE
SALT and PEPPER to taste
MILK to moisten
1 Tbsp. BUTTER

Mix the potatoes and cabbage together. Season well. Add enough milk to moisten, but not wet. Melt the butter in a large skillet until it is very hot, but not brown. Add potatoes and cabbage mixture, pressing down to form a large patty. Fry in butter until the underside is brown, 3 to 5 minutes. Carefully turn and brown until crisp on both sides. Chop roughly with a knife to serve.

Irish Flummery

This is an ancient Celtic recipe from Ireland.
Try it as a dessert even though it is made with oatmeal.

2 oz. SLIVERED ALMONDS
2 oz. quick-cooking OATMEAL
½ pint WHIPPING CREAM
¾ Tbsp. HONEY
½ tsp. LEMON JUICE
1 Tbsp. WHISKEY

Toast the almonds and oatmeal in a skillet until golden brown. Cool completely. Set aside. Beat the cream until thick, not stiff. Fold in remaining ingredients. Add the almonds and oatmeal. Mix well. Spoon into individual dishes. Chill.

Boston Irish Stew

2 lbs. LAMB, cut up into bite-size pieces
FLOUR
OIL
2 14-oz. cans CHICKEN BROTH
SALT and PEPPER to taste
2 ONIONS, chopped
2 CARROTS, sliced
2 BAY LEAVES
6 POTATOES, peeled and quartered
1 Tbsp. FLOUR
1 cup DRY RED WINE

Roll meat in flour. Brown in skillet with oil. In a Dutch oven cover the lamb with chicken broth. Simmer slowly for 1 hour. Add seasoning, onions, carrots and bay leaves. Simmer for another hour. Add potatoes. Simmer for 20 minutes or until potatoes are tender. Remove bay leaves. Make paste with flour. Add to liquid and thicken. Add wine just before serving.

Australain Anzae Biscuits (Cookies)

Submitted by Heather Fanshawe, Queensland, Australia

"This is an Australia and New Zealand Army Corps recipe for a batch of biscuits (cookies) during World War I."

1½ cups quick-cooking OATMEAL
½ cup COCONUT
1½ cups all purpose FLOUR
1 cup SUGAR
1 cup MARGARINE
1 Tbsp. DARK CORN SYRUP
½ tsp. BAKING SODA
¼ cup BOILING WATER
Pinch of SALT

Mix the dry ingredients together. In a saucepan mix the margarine and syrup together. Cook until the margarine is melted. Mix baking soda with boiling water. Add salt. Combine all the ingredients together. Mix well. Place heaping teaspoons of the mixture on a baking tray. Bake in a low oven for 20 minutes. When they cool, they become crisp.

Golden Syrup Dumplings

Submitted by Heather Fanshawe, Queensland, Australia

1¼ cup FLOUR
1 tsp. BAKING POWDER
Pinch CINNAMON
1 Tbsp. BUTTER
4 Tbsp. DARK CORN SYRUP
1/3 cup MILK

Mix ingredients of dumpling batter together. Make the sauce: Heat together 1Tbsp. BUTTER, ¾ cup BROWN SUGAR, 6 Tbsp. DARK CORN SYRUP and 1 ½ cups WATER. Place in bottom of casserole dish. Add the dough mixture by spoonful. Cook in a medium oven for 20 minute. Serve hot with ice cream.

Italian Cheese and Pasta Pie

This is a wonderful dish to impress quests, although it is not some dish you are going to whip up fast. But, it is well worth the time you spend on it.

6 oz. LINGUINI, cooked and drained
1 tsp. OLIVE OIL
2 EGGS, beaten
Greased ALUMINUM FOIL
1 10-oz. pkg. frozen SPINACH, chopped
½ cup SCALLIONS, thinly sliced
¼ cup chopped fresh PARSLEY
1 tsp. BASIL
1 cup COTTAGE CHEESE or
1 cup RICOTTA CHEESE
4 EGGS
½ cup MILK
1 cup shredded MOZZARELLA CHEESE
½ tsp. WORCESTERSHIRE SAUCE
¼ cup PARMESAN CHEESE
SALT and PEPPER to taste

Combine the cooked noodles, olive oil and eggs. Press on the bottom and up the sides of a 10" pie plate to form the crust. Cover the edge of the pasta with the greased foil. Bake in a 375-degree oven for 10 minutes or until the pasta is nice and brown, but not burnt. Set aside. Cook the spinach. Drain and squeeze out the excess water. Put into a bowl. Mix in scallions, parsley and basil. In a large bowl beat together the cheese, rest of eggs and milk. Add half of the mozzarella cheese. Stir in the vegetables, Worcestershire sauce, parmesan cheese and seasoning. Pour into the pasta crust. Sprinkle the remaining mozzarella cheese on top. Bake in a 375-degree oven for 30-35 minutes or until the center comes out clean. Let it rest for 10 minutes before cutting into serving pieces.

Italian Zabaglione

4 EGG YOLKS
1 cup SUGAR
SALT to taste
½ cup DRY SHERRY or MARSALA

Beat the egg yolks in the top of a double boiler. Gradually add sugar and salt, beating all the while. Gradually add sherry. Blend well. Place over gently boiling water. Cook until thickened or until mixture forms soft peaks. Serve in sherbet glasses.

Italian Puffs

2 cups FLOUR
1 tsp. BAKING POWDER
2 EGGS, beaten
1 cup MILK
½ tsp. ORANGE ZEST
½ tsp. VANILLA
VEGETABLE OIL
CONFECTIONER SUGAR

Blend the flour and baking powder in a bowl with a fork. Add eggs, milk and flavoring. Beat well. Heat the oil in a skillet. Drop the batter by spoonful into the hot oil. Fry until puffed and brown on all sides. Drain on paper towels. Roll into confectioner sugar.

Italian Marinade

¾ cup ITALIAN DRESSING
1/3 cup WHITE WINE
2 Tbsp. LEMON JUICE

Mix all together. Refrigerate to blend flavors. Marinate meat, fish or poultry. Reserve ½ cup for basting when cooking.

European Cooking

The countries of German, Poland, Czechoslovakia and other European countries have very substantial food with pork, sausages, cabbage, potatoes, apples, cheese, dark bread and beer.

German Sour Cream Pancakes

1 EGG, beaten
1½ Tbsp. FLOUR
¼ tsp. SALT
2 Tbsp. SOUR CREAM
4 medium-size RUSSET POTATOES
OIL for frying

In a large bowl combine eggs, flour, salt and sour cream. Blend well. Peel potatoes, grate and squeeze dry in a paper towel. Add to egg mixture. Heat the oil and cook the pancakes until brown on both sides. Serve with your favorite sausages.

Czechoslovakian Beer Soup

2 bottles of BEER
1 quart WATER
2 Tbsp. SUGAR
1 Tbsp. BUTTER
3 EGG YOLKS, beaten
1 cup HEAVY CREAM

In a saucepan bring the beer and water to a boil. Add the sugar and butter. Cook on low heat for 30 minutes. In a large bowl beat the eggs with the cream until well blended. Very slowly add the beer mixture. Beat constantly to avoid curdling. Pour back into the saucepan. Heat again slowly. Do not boil.

Hong Kong Egg Drop Soup

2 14.5-oz. cans CHICKEN BROTH
1 Tbsp. thinly sliced CELERY
Few grains of SALT
2 EGG YOLKS

Heat the chicken broth, celery and salt until boiling. Beat egg yolks slightly. Slowly add eggs into the broth, stirring constantly. Let stand a few minutes before serving. Sometimes I add mushrooms.

Russian Potato Salad

4 large RUSSET POTATOES, cooked and cubed
1 ONION, chopped fine
1 stalk CELERY thinly sliced
2 tsp. SUGAR
SALT and PEPPER to taste
½ cup RUSSIAN DRESSING
½ cup MAYONNAISE
1 Tbsp. RED WINE VINEGAR
Bundle of RADISHES, quartered
Sliced cold BEETS

Prepare the potatoes. Mix in the onion and celery. While still warm add the sugar and seasoning. Mix the Russian dressing, mayonnaise and vinegar together. Add to the salad. Chill. Before serving toss in the radishes, adding more dressing if necessary. Serve in a lettuce-lined bowl. Decorate with sliced beets around the top of the bowl.

Scottish Oatcakes

½ cup SHORTENING
1 cup quick-cooking OATMEAL
1 cup FLOUR
1/3 cup SUGAR
½ tsp. BAKING SODA
¼ tsp. SALT
2 to 3 Tbsp. COLD WATER

Cut shortening with dry ingredients until it is fine crumbs. Add a tablespoon of water, one at a time, until it is a soft dough. Roll out on a floured board until 1/8" thick. Cut into squares or rounds. Place on an ungreased cookie sheet. Bake in 350-degree oven for 12 to 15 minutes or until they are brown. Cool on wire rack.

Yorkshire Salad

This is an interesting, easy salad to make and enjoy with its sweet and sour taste. For variety, toss small pieces of Swiss cheese in it.

1 HEAD LETTUCE, shredded
3 SCALLIONS, sliced fine
SALT and PEPPER to taste
3 Tbsp. MOLASSES
6 Tbsp. VINEGAR

Combine the lettuce and scallions in a salad bowl. Toss well. Combine the seasoning with the molasses and vinegar. Pour over the lettuce and toss until well coated. Serve cool, but not icy.

Chinatown Tuna

Submitted by Chang Lee, San Francisco, California

Sauté in 2 Tbsp. MARGARINE, ¼ cup each diced CELERY and chopped ONIONS. Add a 6-oz. can TUNA, a 10 3/4-oz. can of MUSHROOM SOUP and 1 cup of MILK. Heat and simmer for 10 minutes. Serve over Chinese noodles.

J is for Jellied Delights

There are so many tasty and attractive looking combinations of vegetables, fruits, fish and meat that can become a cool salad or side dish as well as a good use of leftovers. A side benefit of gelatin is the nutritional value to your fingernails.

Lime Delight

Try this for a refreshing springtime salad.

1 pkg. LIME-FLAVORED GELATIN
1 cup BOILING WATER
1 cup COLD WATER
1 tsp. MINCED ONION
1½ cups diced CUCUMBER

Dissolve the gelatin in boiling water. Add cold water. Chill to partially set. Stir in onion and cucumber. Chill completely until set. Serve on a bed of lettuce. Garnish with cherry tomatoes. Lemon is also good if you prefer it to lime.

Norwegian Maple Pudding

This is an interesting gelatin desert.

1 Tbsp. UNFLAVORED GELATIN
¼ cup COLD WATER
½ cup MAPLE SYRUP
3 EGG YOLKS, beaten
¼ tsp. MAPLE FLAVORING
½ cup CHOPPED WALNUTS
1 cup HEAVY CREAM, whipped

Soften the gelatin in cold water. Heat the maple syrup to boiling. Add the gelatin. Stir until the mixture is dissolved. In a bowl prepare the egg yolks. Pour the hot syrup over them, beating continuously. Chill until partially set. Add the walnuts. Fold in the whipped cream. Chill in a mold until firm.

Jellied Crab Meat Salad

1 pkg. LEMON-FLAVORED GELATIN
1 cup BOILING WATER
1 8-oz. can TOMATO SAUCE
1 tsp. MINCED ONION
1 Tbsp. sliced CELERY
1 Tbsp. chopped GREEN PEPPER
½ Tbsp. SWEET PICKLE RELISH
SALT and PEPPER to taste
8 oz. CRAB MEAT

In a bowl dissolve the gelatin in the boiling water. Stir in the tomato sauce. Add all of the remaining ingredients. Mix well. Pour into a mold or bowl. Chill and set until firm. For garnish serve Spanish olives with the salad.

This recipe can also be used for shrimp or chopped meats. For ham salad substitute pineapple-flavored gelatin in place of lemon.

Santa Barbara Avocado Mousse

1 tsp GELATIN
½ cup COLD WATER
1 large AVOCADO
½ small ONION, chopped fine
SALT and PEPPER to taste
½ tsp. LEMON JUICE
¼ cup HEAVY CREAM, whipped
4 Tbsp. MAYONNAISE

In a saucepan sprinkle gelatin over cold water. With low heat, stir the gelatin to dissolve. Remove pit from the avocado. Peel and mash the pulp with a fork. Add onion, seasoning and lemon juice. In a bowl mix the whipped cream with mayonnaise. Add gelatin and avocado. Mold in a bowl. Serve with lettuce and tomato wedges.

K is for Kids Corner

Frankfurter Kabobs

BAMBOO SKEWERS
8 FRANKFURTERS
PINEAPPLE CHUNKS
Bite-size MUSHROOM PIECES
OIL

Soak the bamboo skewers in water for 30 minutes. Cut frankfurters into 5 pieces each. Thread the pieces on each skewer alternating with pineapple chunks and mushroom pieces. Brush with oil. Cook on grill for 7 to 10 minutes, turning frequently. Toast the buns. Serve on the buns with barbecue sauce and mustard.

Egg Salad

HARD-COOKED EGGS
SWEET PICKLE RELISH
MUSTARD
MAYONNAISE
SEASONING

Boil the eggs for at least 10 minutes. Shell the eggs while still warm. Do it under a slow running water faucet if they are too warm to handle. Mash the eggs with a fork. Take a fork full of relish, a dab of mustard and enough mayonnaise to mix well. Add salt and pepper to taste. This can be used for a dip with chips or crackers, or a base for a sandwich.

Gelatin Mounds Salad

Make favorite flavored gelatin according to package. Add fruit like fresh strawberries, green or red grapes, sliced peaches or bananas. Spoon into muffin tins and chill. Unmold on a salad plate or in individual bowls with lettuce.

Pizza Snacks

4 ENGLISH MUFFINS
2 Tbsp. MARGARINE
PIZZA SAUCE
4 slices CHEDDAR CHEESE
2 Tbsp. chopped GREEN PEPPER
1 tsp. dried OREGANO
MOZZARELLA CHEESE

Slit each English muffin in half. Sparingly spread each side with margarine. Spread pizza sauce on each piece. Cover with a slice of cheese. Sprinkle green pepper and dried oregano leaves over the cheese. Cover with mozzarella cheese. If you have no oven, cook the pizzas in a skillet with a cover until cheese is melted and cooked through.

Celery Curls

Use the tender, inner stalks of CELERY. Remove all leaves. Cut into 3" long pieces. Slit in the middle lengthwise almost to the end. Chill the stalks in a bowl of ice cubes. When they get really cold, they will curl. Another method is to slit about 1" each side of celery piece so they curl at the edges leaving the middle intact.

Chili Pop Corn

After popping the corn, put it in a large bowl. Mix with 3 Tbsp. melted BUTTER or MARGARINE. Sprinkle with CHILI POWDER and SALT while warm.

Herbed Potato Chips

Spread POTATO CHIPS on a shallow baking dish. Mix ¼ cup grated PARMESAN CHEESE, DILL WEED, THYME and ONION POWDER together. Sprinkle over the chips. Bake in 350-degree oven for 5 minutes.

Cocoa Zucchini Cake

Submitted by Hannah Dean, Brodhead, Wisconsin, age 13

*"I love to cook and made this cake since I was 12.
It is neat to make when it is raining outside."*

2½ cups FLOUR
½ cup UNSWEETENED COCOA
1 tsp. BAKING POWDER
1½ tsp. BAKING SODA
1 tsp. SALT
1 tsp. CINNAMON
¾ cup BUTTER or MARGARINE
2 cups SUGAR
3 EGGS
3 cups finely shredded, unpeeled ZUCCHINI
1 cup chopped WALNUTS
2 tsp. VANILLA
½ cup MILK

Grease and lightly flour a 10' tube pan. Stir together flour, cocoa powder, baking powder, baking soda, salt and cinnamon. In a large mixing bowl, beat butter until well mixed. Add sugar and beat until fluffy. Add eggs, one at a time. Stir in shredded zucchini, nuts and vanilla. Add dry ingredients and milk alternately, beating after each addition. Turn batter into the cake pan. Bake in 350-degree oven for 1 hour or until cake tests done. Cool for 10 minutes. Remove from pan. Cool thoroughly before frosting the cake.

Frosting

Beat together 3-oz. CREAM CHEESE, ½ cup BUTTER and 2 teaspoons VANILLA until fluffy. Gradually add 4 cups of POWDERED SUGAR, beating until smooth. Frost the cake and indulge.

Popeye Breakfast

1 Tbsp. BUTTER
1 10-oz. pkg. frozen SPINACH, drained and chopped
1 cup chopped HAM
4 EGGS, well beaten

In a skillet melt the butter. Add the spinach and ham. Cook together until the ham is hot and the spinach well done. Add the eggs. Cook until eggs are set.

Fruity Dessert

1 pkg. STRAWBERRY-BANANA GELATIN
1 cup BOILING WATER
1 cup COLD WATER
2 BANANAS, sliced
2 ORANGES, peeled and separated into segments
10 STRAWBERRIES, cut in half
Whipped Cream

Put gelatin in a bowl. Pour boiling water over the gelatin. Dissolve. Add cold water. Mix in the fruit. Chill to set. Serve in individual dishes with whipped cream.

Wisconsin Cheddar Cheese Balls

Submitted by Logan Dean, Brodhead, Wisconsin, age 15

"I love to make these and eat them with crackers while I watch television."

16-oz. mild CHEDDAR CHEESE, shredded
8-oz. CREAM CHEESE, softened

Melt the ingredients together in a bowl for 2 minutes in a microwave oven at full power. (If you do not have a microwave, melt it very slowly in a pan on top of a stove.) Form the mixture into a ball. May leave whole or roll it in chopped pecans.

L is for Leftovers

Many a great 'one of a kind' dish can be made by utilizing leftovers. Leftover meats are a good base to which added vegetables, rice, pasta or potatoes can make a meal. Leftover vegetables are a good base to which eggs can be added for breakfast or for lunch. Or use leftover vegetables or fruit for a salad for lunch. Also leftover cold meat or fish make a good salad. Add leftover salad with salsa, cheese and eggs for breakfast. Just use your imagination to create delicious meals.

Leftover rice makes a satisfying breakfast with eggs and bacon. Add the usual onion, scallions, celery, green peppers, tomatoes and/or mushrooms to the rice and make a Spanish dish. Include the rice with the vegetables and egg, or place cooked egg on top.

Ensafada Easy Chili

1 28-oz. can BAKED BEANS, drained
½ cup chopped ONIONS
½ - ¾ cup leftover MEAT, cut into bite-size pieces
½ tsp. CHILI POWDER
1 14.5-oz. can MEXICAN DICED TOMATOES
1 tsp. MUSTARD
GARLIC and PEPPER to taste

Mix together all ingredients in a saucepan and cook slowly to warm up and mellow flavors. Serve with saltine crackers.

Creamed Chicken

Dice leftover CHICKEN into bite-size pieces. Scald in 2 cups of HEAVY CREAM and 1 EGG YOLK, well beaten. Add some SHERRY and SEASONING to taste. Serve over toasted BUNS or bread TOAST. Minced ONION or thinly sliced CELERY can be added to enhance flavor.

Yukon Stew

With canned vegetables and leftover meat, make a delicious stew for lunch or dinner. Beef, pork, fish and poultry are all ideal for a stew. If you have leftover gravy add that to the pot. Be inventive. Peas, carrots, green beans, onions, celery, potatoes, rice or pasta and mushrooms are all great ingredients. Clean out the refrigerator or cooler. Add seasoning. Simmer to blend flavors and enjoy. Serve with French bread or rolls and a salad.

Fish Aspic

Use one large mold or individual molds to serve this aspic.

1 envelop UNFLAVORED GELATIN
½ cup cold CHICKEN BROTH
1 cup hot CHICKEN BROTH
1 Tbsp. SUGAR
½ cup LEMON JUICE
½ tsp. LEMON ZEST
¼ cup each: GREEN PEPPER, ONION, CELERY, CUCUMBER, chopped fine
1 cup cooked, flaked, leftover FISH

In a bowl sprinkle the gelatin in the cold broth. Let stand for 5 minutes. Add hot broth, sugar, lemon juice and zest. Mix well. Cool. Add the vegetables. Pour into the molds and chill. For an added touch serve dry Chinese noodles with it.

Salmon-Spinach Salad

In a large bowl mix cold, cooked SALMON with fresh chopped SPINACH. Set aside. Fry BACON until done and crumble. In the bacon drippings sauté chopped ONION and sliced MUSHROOMS. Add favorite DRESSING or VINEGAR and OIL with HERBS and GARLIC. Mix well and heat through. Pour over salmon and spinach. Toss together. Top with croutons if desired.

Hoppel Poppel

Submitted by Jean Miller Dean, Schenectady, New York

In a skillet melt 4 Tbsp. MARGARINE. Add and fry to brown 3 or 4 diced, leftover cooked POTATOES, ½ lb. of HOT DOGS, sliced, 3 Tbsp. minced ONIONS and SALT and PEPPER to taste. Fry until the potatoes are brown. Break 6 EGGS into the skillet. Stir and continue to fry until eggs are set.

Skillet Supper

"This is a good recipe for leftover potatoes either for supper or breakfast."

—Mary Lou Teetsel, Guilderland, New York

4 or 5 leftover, cold boiled POTATOES, sliced
5 Tbsp. MARGARINE
2 cups HAM cut into bite-size pieces
SALT and PEPPER to taste
4 EGGS, beaten

In a large skillet brown the potatoes in margarine. Add ham and heat through. Sprinkle with seasoning. Add the beaten eggs and stir until the eggs are set.

Jamestown Ham Rolls

1 cup cooked, chopped HAM
¾ cup shredded SWISS CHEESE
2 Tbsp. minced ONIONS
1 EGG
¼ cup BREAD CRUMBS
½ cup MILK
1 cup crushed CORN FLAKES
SHORTENING

Combine the ham, cheese, onions, eggs and crumbs in a bowl. Mix well. Shape into little balls. Dip the balls in the milk and then into the corn flakes. Fry and turn until brown on all sides.

Seventeen Leftover Ideas

1. Add leftover coffee to gravy to make a nice rich, brown color. Make ice cubes of leftover coffee and use when needed.
2. Stir leftover oatmeal into a stew for added flavor and thickening.
3. Store liquid from canned vegetables and mushrooms in the freezer. Use in gravies and soups.
4. To use the last of a ketchup bottle (not more than ¼ cup) add 3 Tbsp. of oil, 1 Tbsp. vinegar, Italian seasoning to make a good salad dressing.
5. Use sweet pickle juice instead of vinegar for cole slaw.
6. Make omelets for breakfast using leftover spaghetti sauce and cheese.
7. Marinate cooked vegetables in French dressing to be used in salads. Italian dressing is good also.
8. Reheat leftover mashed potatoes in a saucepan with a little milk, cheese and onion powder. Or make patties and fry in oil.
9. Use leftover mashed potatoes to top a meatloaf.
10. For leftover rice, mix with chopped green pepper and egg for breakfast. If you have tomatoes, cut up and add to rice. Cook the vegetables until done before adding the eggs. Cook eggs until set.
11. Stuff turkey with a dressing adding leftover chopped meat for a different flavor. Pork is good for this.
12. Serve warmed, leftover stuffing with cold leftover roast. Or heat it in a buttered pan with mushrooms and seasoning.
13. Use leftover vegetables for salad or soups. Keep the water from cooking the vegetables. Make ice cubes of the liquid and use in soups later for added flavor.
14. Use leftover cooked fish with sweet pickle relish, diced cucumber, mayonnaise and lettuce for a delicious sandwich.
15. From leftover ham chop and add to vegetable soup, scrambled eggs or mashed potatoes.
16. When using leftovers have a contrast of colors in the dish to make it more attractive.
17. Lastly, when using leftovers create a dish with contrast in texture to make the dish more interesting.

M is for Munchies

To munch between meals, when traveling or sitting around the campfire consider carrots, apples, celery sticks, popcorn cheese balls or cookies.

Stuffed Celery with Cream Cheese

Cut CELERY into 3" pieces. Mix CREAM CHEESE and chunky PEANUT BUTTER until a nice smooth consistency. Spread into the pieces of celery. Cover and chill.

Fruit Cocktail Cake

Submitted by Sue Clagg, Arroyo Grande, California

- 1½ cup white sugar
- 2 eggs, beaten
- 1 #303 can FRUIT COCKTAIL, undrained
- 2 cups FLOUR (in high altitude add ½ cup more)
- 2 tsp. BAKING SODA
- 1 cup chopped WALNUTS

Mix all ingredients in order given. Pour into baking dish. Bake in a 300-degree oven if using glass and 350-degree oven if in a tin plate.

Make icing: In a saucepan mix ¾ cup SUGAR and 1 cube of MARGARINE together. Add 3/4 cup EVAPORATED MILK. Boil for 2 minutes. Add 1½ cups COCONUT. Spread on cake.

Cinnamon Fry Bread

Thaw a 25-oz. DOUGH LOAVE package. Flatten each roll to 3½" diameter. Heat VEGETABLE OIL in a skillet to 375-degrees. Place rolls in oil. Fry 2 minutes or until brown on the bottom. Turn and brown on other side. Drain on paper towels. Combine ¼ cup SUGAR and 1 Tbsp. CINNAMON. Spread over each piece while hot.

Stuffed Celery

6 stalks CELERY, cut into 3" long pieces
½ cup shredded SWISS CHEESE
½ cup chopped, cooked HAM
½ tsp. MUSTARD
1/3 cup MAYONNAISE

Prepare celery. Mix remaining ingredients. Fill celery cavities. Cover and refrigerate for 1 hour. Decorate with olives.

Scotch Shortbread

1 cup BUTTER
½ cup SUGAR
2 cups FLOUR

Thoroughly cream butter with the sugar, slowly mixing all the time. Beat in the flour a little at a time. Divide the dough in half. Make a ball with the dough. Flatten with hands to make an 8" circle. Place on a greased cookie sheet. Flute the edges. Prick the top with a fork. Bake in a 450-degree oven for 10 minutes or until golden brown. Cut each circle into 8 wedges.

Croutons for Munching

1½ cups spoon-size SHREDDED WHEAT CEREAL
3 Tbsp. BUTTER, melted
½ cup grated PARMESAN CHEESE
SALT and PEPPER to taste

Sauté the cereal in butter for 4 to 6 minutes. Remove from the heat Add the cheese and seasoning. Toss to mix.

Another idea is to use SOURDOUGH BREAD CHUNKS sautéed in butter, adding the cheese and seasoning.

Praline Munchies

1 4-oz. pkg. BUTTERSCOTCH PUDDING MIX
1 cup SUGAR
½ cup BROWN SUGAR
½ cup EVAPORATED MILK
1 Tbsp. BUTTER
½ cup chopped PECANS

In a saucepan combine pudding mix, sugars, milk and butter. Stir and cook over low heat until the soft ball stage. Add nuts. Remove from stove. Beat until it begins to thicken. Drop by spoonful onto wax paper and chill.

Chocolate Oatmeal Cookies

Submitted by Jean Miller Dean, Schenectady, New York

2 cups SUGAR
½ cup COCOA
½ cup MILK
½ cup SHORTENING
3 cups quick-cooking OATMEAL
1 tsp. VANILLA

In a saucepan cook together sugar, cocoa, milk and shortening for 2 minutes or until it comes to a boil. Remove from heat. Add the oatmeal and vanilla. Mix well. Drop by teaspoonful on wax paper or pour into a greased pan. Cut when cold.

Cheese Snacks

Combine 1½ cups BAKING MIX, 1 cup SOUR CREAM, 1 EGG and mix to blend. Stir in 1 cup shredded favorite CHEESE. Bake in 400-degree oven for 10 to 12 minutes until brown. For a Mexican flavor, add some cut-up green CHILIS.

Coconut Bars

2 EGGS, well beaten
2 cups BROWN SUGAR
½ tsp. VANILLA
SALT to taste
2 cups shredded COCONUT
½ cup chopped WALNUT PIECES

Combine in a bowl the ingredients in order given. Pour into an 8" square pan. Bake in a 350-degree oven for 30 minutes. Cool slightly. Cut into bars.

Death Valley Date Bars

1 cup FLOUR
1 tsp. BAKING POWDER
1 tsp. SALT
1 tsp. CINNAMON
1 cup CHOPPEDDATES
1 cup CHOPPED NUTS
3 EGGS, separated
1 cup BROWN SUGAR

In a bowl sift flour, baking powder, salt and cinnamon. Add dates and nuts. Gradually beat egg yolks until thick. Beat in the brown sugar. Add to the flour mixture. Beat egg whites until stiff. Gently fold the eggs into the batter. Pour the batter into a greased and floured 8" square pan. Bake in a 350-degree oven for 30 minutes. Cool. Cut into 1" x 2" bars. Sprinkle confectioner's sugar on top.

Snow Ice Cream

Mama Fowler from Cariboo, B.C. Canada sent in this recipe.

"Catch a bowl of fresh, clean snow. Sweeten with white sugar. Add a flavor of vanilla. Make it pink with coloring or use instant chocolate mix. Children love it."

N is for Noodles

Linguini with Cabbage

1 8-oz. pkg. LINGUINI or FUSILLI
2 Tbsp. BUTTER
½ small head CABBAGE, shredded
½ cup LIGHT CREAM
2 cups shredded SWISS CHEESE
1 tsp. LEMON JUICE
SALT and PEPPER to taste

Cook the pasta in salted boiling water. In a large skillet cook the cabbage until tender over medium heat about 5 minutes. Add the cream. Simmer for 2 minutes. Add cheese. Stir until the cheese is melted. Remove from heat. Add lemon juice and seasoning. Drain pasta when tender. Toss with the cabbage mixture.

Campfire Skillet

Submitted by Jean Miller Dean, Schenectady, New York

1 12-oz. can TOMATOES
3 cups WATER
2 Tbsp. PARSLEY FLAKES
SALT to taste
½ tsp. BASIL
¼ tsp. GARLIC POWDER
Dash PEPPER
1 8-oz.pkg. medium-size EGG NOODLES
1 10-oz. can HOT DOGS
¼ cup grated AMERICAN CHEESE

In a large skillet combine tomatoes, water, parsley and seasonings. Bring to a boil. Add noodles. Cook, covered until tender, stirring occasionally. Add hot dogs. Sprinkle with cheese. Heat through.

Fettucine Alfredo

1 8-oz.pkg. SPINACH FETTUCINE NOODLES
Salted BOILING WATER
¼ cup OIL
2 Tbsp. Chopped Fresh BASIL
¼ lb. SWEET BUTTER, cubed
¾ cup grated PARMESAN CHEESE
¼ cup HEAVY CREAM, warmed
½ tsp. PEPPER

Cook the fettuccine in water and oil until tender. Drain. Place in a bowl. Add basil, butter, cheese, cream and pepper. Toss together.

Arcata Stuffed Pasta Shells

1 12-oz. pkg. JUMBO PASTA SHELLS
½ lb. RICOTTA CHEESE
2 cups shredded MOZZARELLA CHEESE
1 10-oz. pkg. frozen SPINACH, thawed, drained and
¼ cup chopped ONIONS   chopped
1 28-oz. jar SPAGHETTI SAUCE
Strips of GREEN PEPPER

Cook pasta shells for 5 minutes in salted boiling water. Drain. Set aside. Combine cheeses with spinach and onions. Stuff into the shells. Place the shells in the bottom of a greased 13"x 9" x 2" baking pan. Pour spaghetti sauce over all. Decorate with pepper strips. Bake in 350-degree oven for 45 minutes, or until done.

Sauteed Noodles

Cook 8-oz. NOODLES in salted boiling water. Dry thoroughly on paper towels. In a skillet melt 4 Tbsp. BUTTER. Add noodles. Toss over medium heat and brown. Add MOZZARELLA CHEESE. Sprinkle dry basil over the noodles while hot. Use as a base for creamed chicken, ham and other meats.

Lasagna

9 pieces LASAGNA NOODLES
Salted BOILING WATER
1 28-oz. jar SPAGHETTI SAUCE with MEAT
1 lb. COTTAGE CHEESE or RICOTTA CHEESE
1 10-oz. frozen SPINACH, drained and chopped
Strips of GREEN PEPPER
MOZZARELLA CHEESE

In a large pot cook the lasagna noodles in the water for 5 minutes. Drain. Spread a thin layer of sauce in the bottom of a baking pan. In a row lay 3 noodles. Spread 1/3 of cheese over the noodles. Spread ½ of spinach over cheese. Spread 1/3 sauce over spinach. Make second layer. On the last layer do not add any spinach. Cover the noodles with the remaining sauce and mozzarella cheese. Decorate with green pepper. Bake in a 350-degree oven for 1 hour or until done. Let stand 15 minutes before serving.

Fried Noodle Chips

½ lb. thin-size NOODLES
2 cups VEGETABLE OIL
1 tsp. BASIL
PARMESAN CHEESE, optional

Boil the noodles 5 to 6 minutes in salted boiling water or until done. Rinse in a colander with cold water. Add 2 Tbsp. oil and basil to noodles. Toss to blend. Place remaining oil in a skillet. Fry noodles, a few at a time, to a delicate brown. Drain on paper towels. For added flavor, sprinkle parmesan cheese on top.

MEASUREMENTS

2 ounces per person of dry SPAGHETTI serves as a main dish.

Allow 4 ounces of MACARONI serving 3 as a main dish.

Baked Macaroni and Cheese

Sometimes homemade tastes better than Krafts.
If you are cooking for children, try wagon wheel macaroni instead of elbow.

1 9-oz.pkg.ELBOW MACARONI
1 cup shredded CHEDDAR CHEESE
4 Tbsp. BUTTER
4 Tbsp. FLOUR
2 cups cold MILK
SALT and PEPPER to taste
½ cup buttered HERB BREAD CRUMBS
MONTEREY JACK CHEESE, optional
Strips of GREEN PEPPER

Cook the macaroni in the salted boiling water. Drain. Place ½ of the macaroni in the bottom of a buttered baking dish. Sprinkle with ½ of cheddar cheese. Cover with the rest of the macaroni and the cheese. Set aside. In a saucepan melt the butter. Add flour. Blend well over low heat. Stir in milk and seasoning. Whisk until a boiling point. Cook 2 minutes. Spread over the macaroni and cheese. Top with bread crumbs. Sprinkle jack cheese on the top. Decorate with green pepper. Bake in a 350-degree oven for 4-5 minutes or until brown.

Viennese Noodles

1 8-oz. pkg. thin NOODLES
¼ cup BUTTER
½ cup BLANCHED ALMONDS, coarsely chopped
2 tsp. POPPYSEEDS
SEASONING to taste

Cook noodles in salted boiling water until tender. Drain. Melt a tablespoon of butter in a large skillet. Add almonds. Stir over low heat until light brown. Add noodles and remaining ingredients. Stir well until thoroughly heated. Serve with chicken or pork.

O is for On-the-Trail

The clear air, blue skies; gnarly, green foxtail pines; white granite rocks; sparkling blue lakes; morning or evening rosy-glow on the nearby mountains and a campfire. The end of a perfect day in the high country. With a full moon at night, it is heaven. You can enjoy it all. It only takes planning—how many pounds you can carry and how many days out.

A knowledge of botany is helpful to locate wild plants for enhancing and supplementing the diet. Wild onion, garlic bulbs, clover or dandelion leaves, sorrel and watercress add flavor to stews and chowders. Although clover leaves are not significant in taste, they have high nutritional value.

Plan each meal carefully. Make detailed menus. Prepare plastic bags with amounts for the number of people and the number of meals needed. Count out the amount of instant rice, lentils, pasta, orzo, potato flakes, onion powder or dry onion flakes, dried fruits and vegetables, oatmeal, cornmeal, nuts and powdered milk. Grated parmesan cheese keeps well. Bulk cheese like cheddar, Monterey Jack, Swiss or processed cheese lasts about a week, as does bacon. Eggs stay unbroken in their plastic holders.

Make up packets for prepared biscuit and cake mixes, pancake flour, cracker meal and dried herbed bread crumbs. They make a good substitute for coating the fish. Add paprika to some bread crumbs as they make the fish browner.

Fortunately there is plenty of water. Check supermarkets, sports stores and mountain shops for dried foods like soups, granola and fruits. There is a large variety of instant soups to use as a base for a meal. If you plan to carry those prepared dinners, that sound so good on the package, but in reality are not the best, try them out at home to see which brand you prefer for taste and texture. Some are too salty with too many calories.

Instant puddings and gelatins make great desserts. Use dry milk. Add nuts, raisins, dried fruit that has been soaked in water and softened. To cool set in the nearby stream or lake. When we were in the high country we made pancakes for breakfast and enough cakes for lunch. We put jelly and peanut butter on them, rolled them up for sandwiches so we didn't have to set up camp for lunch. Cheese with tortillas are great, also tasty and easy.

Salt is important to include as it is good for added flavor as well as to replace the salt drained from the body through perspiration. Salt tablets added to water helps relieve headaches and nausea from high altitude. It is said that garlic consumption discourages mosquitoes from biting.

Be sure to take a flat grill to lay on rocks over a campfire. Take a single burner stove, reflector oven, skillet with a cover, a multi-duty saucepan and a larger pan for water. Don't forget the collapsible cup to carry on the belt for drinking water.

High Altitude Cooking

Cooking time usually doubles with the boiling point one-degree for every 550 feet rise in elevation. Simmer is a good term for cooking as the food cooks from 135 to 160 degrees F.

Sugar and grease become hotter and burn faster. Baking powder or baking soda increases the lightness of texture when baked. For each teaspoon of baking powder or baking soda, when making the biscuit mixes, decrease by ¼ teaspoon. For each cup of liquid increase by 2 tablespoons. If using an oven, increase by 25 degrees.

Use plastic packets for kitchen utensils, silverware, matches, tea, coffee, clothespins and rope. Put soaps, toiletries, vitamins and pills in zippered plastic bags. Take small plastic bottles of honey, ketchup, mustard, mayonnaise, and relish. Include a small plastic tablecloth, paper plates, paper towels, aluminum foil and candles.

Some Tips On Camping

1. Include snack foods like granola bars for hiking and climbing.
2. Use empty plastic bags for trash to go out with you. Remember what you take in must go out, except what paper can be burned. Crush cans flat when empty for easy travel.
3. Take any cooking instructions necessary.
4. Include wooden spoon, spatula, kitchen tongs and can opener, if you plan to use canned foods.
5. Fels-Naphtha soap is good for washing and soothes mosquito bites and poison ivy rash.
6. Take chlorine tablets to sterilize water.
7. Take an extra day amount of food for emergencies.
8. Salami and jerky are a good source of protein and travel well.
9. Margarine keeps better then butter. It also tastes better than oil.
10. Baking soda is a must to carry for its many uses. Read up on the many benefits medicinally before you go.

Hot Chocolate Mix

½ lb. CHOCOLATE-FLAVORED DRINK MIX
4 quarts DRY MILK
1½ cups POWDERED SUGAR
1 cup NON-DAIRY COFFEE CREAMER

Combine all ingredients in a bowl. Mix well. Store in a plastic container. At camp fill a cup 1/3 full with dry mix. Add hot water. Stir and enjoy. Marshmallows are good with it. Makes 20 servings.

Camp Coffee

Put enough coffee grounds or instant coffee in a plastic container for the trip. Measure out the amount needed for a cup and heat the water on the campfire or stove. Cook the grounds for 5 minutes but just boil the water for instant coffee. Take packets of sugar and creamer if needed.

Basic Biscuit Mix

This recipe is for 10 cups of mix. Measure out how much you will need and make the mix up accordingly.

8 cups FLOUR
1½ cups DRY MILK
¼ cup BAKING POWDER
SALT

Mix together and put in a plastic bag well marked. In camp add a Tbsp. of margarine and water to a cup of mix. Mix in grated cheese, raisins and some cinnamon. Bake in skillet on stove top.

Pancake Mix

This recipe is for one batch of 6 cakes. Double, triple or whatever you need for the trip.

1 cup BAKING MIX
2 tsp. SUGAR
1/3 cup EGG POWDER
¼ cup DRY MILK

Mix together and put in a plastic bag well marked. In camp add water and cook in the skillet.

Pudding Mix

2 cups DRY MILK
1 cup SUGAR
¾ cups CORNSTARCH
½ tsp. SALT

At home mix completely. Place in plastic bag, well marked. In camp add 2 cups water. Boil gently for 3 minutes. For chocolate use pieces of a chocolate bar or chocolate bits. For butterscotch pudding add butterscotch morsels. Use ¼" vanilla bean (found in seasoning department in market) and 2 Tbsp. margarine for vanilla.

Trail Mix

2 lbs. CASHEW NUTS
2 lbs. ROASTED PEANUTS
1 lb. M&M candy
1 lb. RAISINS
½ lb. flaked COCONUT

Mix all together. Place in individual plastic sandwich bags.

Granola

2 cups OATMEAL
1 cup of shredded FLAKED COCONUT
1 cup WHEAT GERM
1 cup SUNFLOWER SEEDS
1 cup HONEY
½ cup RAISINS
½ cup SLIVERED ALMONDS
½ cup SESAME SEEDS
½ cup chopped WALNUTS
½ cup SALAD OIL

Combine all ingredients in a mixing bowl. Thoroughly blend. Spread on baking sheet. Bake in 325-degree oven for 20 minutes, stirring so as not to burn. Cool. Store in plastic bags to carry.

Another version is to add 1/3 cup BROWN SUGAR and 2 tsp. VANILLA EXTRACT for a sweeter taste.

Peanut Balls

Mix and form into balls 1 cup chopped PEANUTS, ½ cup HONEY, 1 cup DRY MILK. Roll into POWDERED SUGAR, crushed CORN FLAKES or crushed PECANS.

Eastern Clam Chowder

1 pkg. dry CHICKEN NOODLE SOUP
3½ cups BOILING WATER
½ cup DRY MILK
1 8-oz. can MINCED CLAMS

Cook as directed on soup package, adding milk and clams.

For a hearty chicken soup add a 10-oz. can of WHITE CHICKEN MEAT instead of clams, with some dried vegetables.

Make a fish chowder from leftover trout. Use above recipe and add chopped trout in place of clams. Add dry vegetables for more nourishment. For extra goodness make dumplings.

EASY DUMPLINGS: Use BAKING MIX with DRY MILK, adding enough water for a stiff dough. Drop by spoonful into hot chowder liquid. Cook uncovered for 10 minutes and covered for 10 minutes. Check the time as it may be longer in high altitude.

Fresh Vegetables

Fresh vegetables can be carried in plastic bags. Wash and clean at home. Dry. BABY CARROTS and CELERY stalks are great for munching. CABBAGE, GREEN PEPPERS and CUCUMBER are good and keep well. Cook them, cut up in a skillet, with margarine. For soups and stews use dried ONIONS or ONION POWDER, dried VEGETABLES, especially dried TOMATOES.

Rice, Orzo, Lentil and Pasta

These are stable foods to cook in salted boiling water. Mix with dried vegetables, dried mushrooms, dry soup mixes, salami or fish to make a satisfying meal. Add cheese for more nourishment.

POTATOES: Use instant potatoes with margarine, cheese and dry milk. Make a stiff batter and fry in a skillet like griddle cakes.

Bouillon Beef Stew

BOILING WATER
1 cube BEEF BOUILLON
1 pkg. dried VEGETABLES
1 pkg. ONION SOUP MIX
4 BABY CARROTS, cut in half
3 stalks CELERY, sliced

In boiling water dissolve bouillon cube. Add dried vegetables, onion soup mix, carrots and celery. Cook until done.

Cooked Cucumber

Instead of serving sliced cucumber in a salad, cook it. In a skillet cook thin slices of cucumber in beef or chicken bouillon for 5 to 8 minutes, or until tender. Season with margarine and pepper. With bouillon there is no need for salt.

No-Bake Cookies

Submitted by Jean Miller Dean, Schenectady, New York

3 cups quick-cooking OATMEAL
½ cup COCONUT
½ cup chopped NUTS
4 Tbsp. CHOCOLATE-FLAVORED DRINK MIX
½ cup DRY MILK
½ cup MARGARINE
½ cup WATER

Mix the oatmeal, coconut, nuts, drink mix and dry milk at home. The mix has enough sweetener in it so no sugar is required. Taste to adjust the sugar content. At night in camp melt the margarine in water. Cool and add to the dry ingredients. Mix well. Drop by spoonful on a piece of foil. Act quickly as it sets up fast. Serve these with the pudding around the campfire.

Pan Onion Biscuits

1½ cups BAKING MIX
½ cup CORNMEAL
½ tsp. dry ONION FLAKES
½ cup DRY MILK
2 Tbsp. MARGARINE, melted
½ cup WATER
2 Tbsp. MARGARINE

Combine baking mix and cornmeal. Add onion flakes, milk and margarine. Add enough water to make a good dough. On a flat, floured surface knead the dough about 10 times. Make into balls, then flatten to form a biscuit 2" thick. Melt the margarine in a skillet. Add biscuits. Cook until browned on both sides.

Other ideas for biscuits are: add raisins, nuts, oatmeal, wheat germ, honey and cheese. Biscuits are good with dinner, breakfast and lunch. Make a batch at night in a skillet with the campfire for the next day. With different flavors they are always tasty.

Bannock

Submitted by Edna and Alec Farquharson, Kamloops, B.C. Canada

2½ cups FLOUR
¼ cup SKIM MILK POWDER
2 EGGS
4 tsp, BAKING POWDER
½ tsp. SALT
1 tsp. melted SHORTENING
¾ cup WATER to make a non-sticky dough

Mix all ingredients. Flatten to about 1" thick. Fry on a HOT, greased fry pan to golden brown. Flip over to brown other side. Stand bannock in front of the fire to brown.

P is for Potato

Potato Candy

2/3 cups MASHED POTATOES (can use instant potato)
1 square UNSWEETENED CHOCOLATE, melted
1 tsp. INSTANT COFFEE
¼ tsp. SALT
1 lb. CONFECTIONER'S SUGAR, sifted
½ lb. shredded COCONUT

Combine mashed potatoes with chocolate, coffee and salt. Add sugar. Work in coconut until well blended. Form into balls. Drop on to a cookie sheet lined with waxed paper. Refrigerate 3 to 4 hours until hardened.

Red Potato Salad

Submitted by Wendy Sara-May Miller, Peoria, Arizona

4 cups diced, cooked RED POTATOES
3 HARD-COOKED EGGS
½ cup chopped RED ONION
½ cup chopped CELERY
¼ cup SWEET PICKLE RELISH
2/3 cup MAYONNAISE
1 Tbsp. RED WINE VINEGAR
1 tsp. dry MUSTARD
¼ cup OLIVE OIL
SALT and PEPPER to taste
CUCUMBER SLICES

In a bowl mix potatoes with 2 of the hard-cooked eggs, chopped. Add onion, celery and relish. Gently blend. Add remaining ingredients except the 3rd egg. Mix well. Place in a serving bowl on a bed of lettuce. Decorate with sliced egg on top of salad. Surround with slices of cucumber.

Creamed Potato Bake

1 lb. Idaho POTATOES, peeled and quartered
½ cup MELTED BUTTER
2 cups LIGHT CREAM
½ Tbsp. POWDERED ONION
¼ tsp. CELERY SALT
PEPPER to taste
1/3 cup BREAD CRUMBS
1/3 cup PARMESAN CHEESE
MELTED BUTTER
Strips of GREEN PEPPER

In a medium saucepan cover the potatoes with water. Boil until tender. You may want to cook the potatoes first, then peel. Chill, covered, at least 4 hours or overnight. In a large saucepan mix the melted butter, cream, onion powder and seasoning. Cook until thickened. Stir occasionally so it doesn't burn. Spoon potatoes into a buttered baking pan. Spread bread crumbs on the top. Drizzle cheese over crumbs. Place the melted butter over all. Decorate with strips of green pepper. Bake in a 350-degree oven until brown and bubbly, about 45-50 minutes.

For a simpler version, use a can of 14.5 oz. WHOLE WHITE POTATOES. Cook the melted butter, cream, onion powder and seasonings until thick. Follow rest of recipe.

Deluxe Mashed Potatoes

1 3¼-oz. pkg. INSTANT MASHED POTATOES
½ cup SOUR CREAM
SALT and PEPPER to taste
SWISS CHEESE, shredded

Prepare potatoes as directed on package, omitting the butter. Stir in sour cream and seasoning. Heat through. Melt cheese on top.

Fried Potatoes

Submitted by Ian and Audrey McKenzie, Kamloops, B.C, Canada

Peel enough potatoes For Your Group And Cut Into Cubes. Put These Into A Frying Pan With Enough Bacon To Fry Nicely. When The Potatoes Are Well Cooked, Add A Few Eggs. Cook A Few Minutes Longer For The Eggs To Set. Season To Taste Salt And Pepper.

Scottish Potato Cakes

Submitted by Ian and Audrey McKenzie, Kamloops. B.C, Canada

2 cups cold, cooked MASHED POTATOES
1 cup FLOUR
SALT to taste
Big lump of MELTED BUTTER
MILK

Combine potatoes and flour. Add salt and butter. Mix well. Moisten with milk to bind. Roll out on a floured board. Cut into squares or triangular shapes. Place into a warm fry pan with melted butter or bacon fat. Fry until nicely brown on both sides.

Wichita Skillet Potato Pie

6 slices BACON
1 medium ONION, chopped
¼ cup chopped GREEN PEPPER
1 9-oz. pkg. frozen FRENCH FRIED POTATOES
6 EGGS
½ cup MILK
SALT and PEPPER to taste
PARSLEY

Cook bacon until crisp. Crumble into bits. Set aside. Cook onions, green pepper and potatoes in bacon fat. Discard excess fat. Beat eggs, milk and seasoning. Pour over potatoes. Sprinkle bacon and parsley over egg. Cover. Cook over low heat until eggs are set.

Q is for Quick and Easy

Quick and Easy Cheese Sandwich

Directions are for a single serving.
This is an easy, fast food for breakfast or lunch with soup.

2 slices favorite BREAD (sourdough is great with this)
BUTTER
1 thick slice SWISS, CHEDDAR OR
MONTEREY JACK CHEESE

Toast the bread. Butter. Place the cheese on one side of toast and cover with the other. Microwave for 25 seconds or until the cheese is melted. Cut into fourths. If you have no microwave oven, place in a buttered skillet and brown the toast until cheese is melted.

Cornmeal Cake or Muffins

This is good with a pork dinner instead of rolls or for breakfast with coffee.
Heat slightly if using as a leftover.

1 box of CORNMEAL MUFFIN MIX
1 cup shredded CHEDDAR CHEESE
1 cup canned creamed or kernel CORN

Follow the directions on the mix package to prepare the dough. Add the cheese and corn to the batter. The type of corn is for individual taste. Instead of water to mix the dough, use the corn liquid to moisten the batter. Pour into a greased 8" square pan. Bake at 350-degree oven for 20 minutes or until brown.

Cornmeal Griddle Cakes

To the cornmeal mix add 2 tbsp. of melted MARGARINE, ½ cup of MILK and ½ cup of shredded CHEDDAR CHEESE. Mix together. It is best to make small cakes as it is not as easy to turn as regular griddle cakes. Serve with jam or syrup.

Quick and Easy Crumb Cake

3 cups FLOUR
2 cups SUGAR
2 tsp. BAKING POWDER
½ tsp. SALT
½ cup MARGARINE
2 EGGS
1 cup MILK
1 tsp. CINNAMON

Sift together flour, sugar, baking powder and salt. Work in margarine for a crumbly dough. Set aside 1 cup of crumb mixture. Add the eggs and milk to the batter. Beat together. Pour into a shallow buttered pan. Mix cinnamon with the crumb mixture. Spread on top of batter. Bake in a 350-degree oven for 20 minutes or until done.

Great Tomato-Chicken Salad

1½ cups chopped cooked CHICKEN
½ cup chopped CELERY
½ cup chopped ONION
¼ cup chopped WALNUTS
1/3 cup MAYONNAISE
2 Tbsp. SWEET PICKLE RELISH
SALT and PEPPER to taste
4 large, whole TOMARANCH SALAD DRESSING
TOES

Combine all ingredients except tomatoes and salad dressing. Cut the tops off tomatoes. Scoop out pulp to make a shell. Stuff the chicken mixture into the shells. Chop and mix the pulp from the tomatoes with the dressing. Pour over the tomatoes.

Boiled Dinner

1 14.5-oz. can GREEN BEANS
1 14.5-oz. can SLICED CARROTS
1 14.5-oz. can WHITE WHOLE POTATOES, drained
8 SAUSAGES
1 small CABBAGE, shredded
1 Tbsp. dry ONIONS
SALT and PEPPER to taste

Place green beans and carrots with their liquid in the bottom of a saucepan or a Dutch oven. Place potatoes on top. Slit the sausages diagonally about ¼" deep. Place on top of potatoes. Place cabbage over meat. Sprinkle onions and seasoning over all. Heat to boiling. Cover and simmer until sausages is cooked and cabbage is tender.

Boston Baked Beans

1 28-oz. can BAKED BEANS, drained
¼ cup chopped ONIONS
2 Tbsp. MAPLE SYRUP
2 Tbsp. BROWN SUGAR
1 Tbsp. MUSTARD

Place all ingredients into a saucepan. Slowly heat. Serve with saltine crackers or cornbread.

Chocolate Pie

2 cups CHOCOLATE CRUMBS (from wafer cookies)
¾ cup chopped WALNUTS
½ cup melted BUTTER
1 envelope CHOCOLATE PUDDING MIX
WHIPPED CREAM
CRUMBLED WALNUTS
STRAWBERRIES, optional

If you don't have a blender to make the crumbs from the chocolate cookies, put cookies in a plastic bag and seal. With rolling pin crush the cookies. To the crumbs add walnuts and butter. Press into the bottom of a pie pan and sides to form the crust. Bake 8 minutes in a 375-degree oven. Cool.

Mix the pudding according to directions on the package for pie. Pour into the cooled baked shell. When serving top with whipped cream and walnuts. Be fancy and add strawberries.

Quick Glouster Clam Casserole

1 10-oz. can BABY CLAMS, chopped
2 EGGS, beaten
1 10.5-oz. can CREAM MUSHROOM SOUP
1 cup MILK
SALT and PEPPER to taste
30 SALTINE CRACKERS, crushed

Mix all into a casserole dish. Bake at 350-degree oven for an hour.

Chicken or Turkey Rolls

1 cup diced, cooked CHICKEN or TURKEY
¾ cup thinly sliced CELERY
½ of 4-oz. can MUSHROOMS, chopped
1 tsp. diced ONIONS
1 tsp. LEMON JUICE
SALT and PEPPER to taste
1 Tbsp. MAYONNAISE
1 Tbsp. grated CHEDDAR CHEESE
4 FRENCH ROLLS

Combine everything but the rolls. Scoop out the center of the rolls. Fill each shell with the chicken mixture. Wrap each roll in foil. Place on grill. Heat 20-25 minutes turning occasionally.

R is for Rice

Green Rice

1 9-oz. pkg. frozen SPINACH
1 7-oz. pkg. CHICKEN-FLAVORED RICE
2 Tbsp. MARGARINE
1¾ cups BOILING WATER
SALT and PEPPER to taste
Dash NUTMEG

Prepare the spinach. Cook the rice with margarine, water and seasoning as per directions on package. Combine spinach, rice and nutmeg in a large bowl. Mix well. Spoon into a 4-cup ring mold to be fancy, or leave it in the bowl. Let stand in a warm place for 5 minutes. Unmold onto a warm serving dish.

Rice Stuffing for Trout

1½ cup cooked RICE
½ cup chopped ONION
1 stalk CELERY, chopped
¼ cup sliced MUSHROOMS
2 Tbsp. BUTTER
1 tsp. GARLIC & HERB SEASONING
¾ cup CHICKEN BROTH
¼ cup WHITE WINE

Mix the first 6 ingredients in a bowl. Combine with the broth and wine. Mix well. Stuff the whole fish. Wrap in foil. Grill until the fish is cooked.

Rice Side Dish

In a flavored rice package enhance the dish by adding chopped onion, canned tomato, chopped green pepper and mushrooms.

Newport Rice Pudding

1 quart MILK
3 Tbsp. RICE
½ cup SUGAR
½ tsp. SALT
2 EGGS, beaten
1/3 cup RAISINS
1 tsp. VANILLA
1 Tbsp. BUTTER

In a saucepan combine milk, rice, sugar and salt. Cook slowly for 1½ hours. If using instant rice, cook until done. Slowly add the eggs and raisins. Cook 3 minutes. Add vanilla and butter. Blend.

Rice Dessert

1 cup WHIPPING CREAM
½ cup SUGAR
1 cup FRUIT COCKTAIL MIX
2 cups cooked RICE

Whip the cream until stiff. Slowly add sugar while beating. Mix the fruit with the rice. Fold into whipped cream. Chill. Serve cold.

Lancaster Brown Rice

1 cup BROWN RICE
1 cup finely sliced CELERY
¾ cup chopped ONION
½ of 4-oz. can MUSHROOM
SALT and PEPPER to taste
1 14.5-oz. can BEEF BROTH

Cook the rice, celery, onion, mushrooms and seasoning until all liquid is absorbed. If more liquid is necessary because the rice is not done, add more water a little at a time.

Mexican Rice

2 cups RICE
2 Tbsp. MARGARINE
2 14.5-oz. cans BEEF BROTH
½ cup chopped ONIONS
½ cup sliced CELERY
½ cup chopped GREEN PEPPER
1 cup frozen PEAS
1 14.5-oz. can MEXICAN STEWED TOMATOES
½ tsp. GARLIC SALT
¼ tsp. CHILI POWDER

In a large skillet cook the rice in margarine until golden brown. Add ½ cup of broth, onion, celery and green pepper. Sauté 2 minutes. Stir in remaining ingredients. Bring to a boil. Reduce heat. Cover and simmer for 20-25 minutes until all broth is absorbed. If any rice is leftover, reheat for breakfast with egg.

Risotto

3 Tbsp. BUTTER
2 Tbsp. OLIVE OIL
1 cup RICE
1 small ONION, finely chopped
1 clove GARLIC, minced
½ of 4-oz. can MUSHROOMS
2 14.5-oz. cans CHICKEN BROTH
Pinch of SAGE and BASIL
½ cup WHITE WINE
½ cup PARMESAN CHEESE

Heat butter and oil in a large skillet. Sauté rice until golden brown. Add onion, garlic and mushrooms. Blend well. Add broth and seasoning. Cover and cook 15 minutes. Add wine. Cook until all liquid is absorbed and rice is cooked. Add parmesan cheese. Serve.

S is for Seafood

New England Clam and Tomato Bisque

1 10-oz. can CLAMS
1 10.5 -oz. can TOMATO SOUP
1 soup can WATER
1 tsp. LEMON JUICE
SALT and PEPPER to taste
PARSLEY

Heat clams with liquid, tomato soup, water, lemon juice and seasoning. Bring to a boil, then simmer for 5 minutes. Serve into bowls. Sprinkle parsley on top. Serve with saltine crackers.

Pioneer Chowder

Submitted by Marion Freisatz, Guilderland, New York

"This recipe is good with clams and chicken as well as shrimp."

1 medium ONION, sliced thin
½ cup thinly sliced CELERY
2 Tbsp. MARGARINE
2 10.5-oz.cans CREAM OF POTATO SOUP
1½ soup can of MILK
1 15.25-oz. can WHOLE KERNAL CORN
1 lb. cooked SHRIMP
½ tsp. SALT
1 cup CREAM or MILK

Sauté onion and celery in butter for 5 minutes. Add soup, milk, corn, shrimp and salt. Cook and stir over low heat until it comes to a boil. Stir in cream or milk. Stir until mixture comes to a boil.

Fried Oysters

Combine 1 EGG with 1 tsp. MILK. Dip OYSTERS in the egg. Roll in HERBED BREAD CRUMBS. Fry in HOT FAT for 2 minutes.

Sweet and Sour Scallops

This recipe is also good with jumbo shrimp.

2 lbs. JUMBO SCALLOPS
½ cup finely chopped ONIONS
½ cup BROWN SUGAR
¼ cup MELTED BUTTER
2 tsp. MUSTARD
½ tsp. PAPRIKA
SALT and PEPPER to taste
Strips of GREEN PEPPER
Chunks of PINEAPPLE

Defrost scallops if frozen. Wipe dry. In a large bowl mix onions, brown sugar, butter, mustard, paprika and seasoning. Add scallops. Mix to coat scallops. Refrigerate to marinate the scallops for 2 hours at least. Grill over hot coals for 10 minutes each side. Serve with green peppers and chunks of pineapple.

Crab Pitas

½ lb. CRAB MEAT
5 Tbsp. MAYONNAISE
¼ cup plain YOGURT
½ tsp. LEMON ZEST
¼ cup sliced GREEN ONION
½ cup diced TOMATOES
½ cup chopped, unpeeled CUCUMBER
¼ cup thinly sliced CELERY
4 PITA BREAD
4 pieces LEAF LETTUCE

In a bowl combine and mix thoroughly all ingredients except bread and lettuce. Cover and chill in refrigerator. Split the pita bread about 1/3 of circumference. Insert a leaf of lettuce. Fill with crab salad. Serve with Spanish olives.

Scrumptious Shrimp Spread

Submitted by Maggie Parker, Lake Havasu City, Arizona

1 envelop UNFLAVORED GELATIN
½ cup COLD WATER
1 8-oz. pkg. CREAM CHEESE, softened
1 10.5-oz. can TOMATO SOUP
1 medium ONION, finely chopped
1 cup finely chopped CELERY
1 cup MAYONNAISE
2 6-oz. cans TINY SHRIMP or
12-oz. cooked SALAD SHRIMP

Sprinkle gelatin over cold water; dissolve over low heat. Combine softened cream cheese, soup and onion. Cook over low heat until smooth. Remove from heat. Add remaining ingredients. Mix well. Pour into a greased 4-cup mold or 8" x 8" pan. Chill 4 to 6 hours. Unmold on platter. Serve with crackers.

Options: Chopped CUCUMBER, plus 2 tsp. DILL WEED

And/or chopped WATER CHESTNUTS.

Boiled Lobster Tails

1 LOBSTER TAIL per serving
Boiling SALTED WATER
MELTED BUTTER
½ tsp. LEMON JUICE

Cover tail and cook in boiled water 5 minutes. Serve as is with lemon and melted butter. Or use as meat in other dishes.

Cut cooked LOBSTER MEAT in large pieces. Mix with LEMON JUICE and SALT and PEPPER. Dip in BREAD CRUMBS, then into a well-beaten EGG. Again in bread crumbs. Fry in deep fat. Drain. Serve with tarter sauce, page 29.

Lobster Spread

Chop cooked LOBSTER MEAT. Add chopped HARD-COOKED EGGS, finely chopped CELERY, finely chopped ONION and chopped unpeeled CUCUMBER. Combine with mayonnaise. Season to taste. Use for a sandwich spread or on crackers for appetizers. If you have pimientos, mince them and add to the spread.

Seafood Salad

½ lb. medium-size cooked SHRIMP
1 cup cooked flaked CRAB
1 cup chopped CELERY
¼ cup SWEET PICKLE RELISH
2 Tbsp. LEMON JUICE
½ cup MAYONNAISE

Combine all ingredients in a large bowl. Chill several hours to meld flavors. Serve on a bed of lettuce with a dill pickle.

Crabmeat Chowder

1 medium ONION, finely diced
4 stalks CELERY, finely diced
2 cups diced POTATOES
3 cups BEEF BOUILLON
1 pint MILK
1 pint CREAM
1 quart fresh CRAB MEAT
SALT and PEPPER to taste
1 cup SHERRY

In a large kettle cook onions, celery and potatoes in bouillon until tender. Add milk, cream, crabmeat and seasoning. Heat through. Add sherry. Serve piping hot with saltine crackers.

T is for Tex-Mex Dishes

Carne Molida Con Queso (hamburger with cheese)

1½ lbs. GROUND BEEF
1 tsp. SALT
1/3 cup DRY RED WINE
1 small ONION, chopped fine
4 cubes SHARP CHEDDAR CHEESE

Mix first four ingredients. Form meat mixture into 8 patties. Put a cube of cheese on top of 4 patties. Place the remaining patties on top of cheese. Seal edges of patties. Slightly flatten the patties. Grill over hot coals for 5 to 6 minutes. Test for doneness.

Taco Tureen

Submitted by Jean Miller Dean, Schenectady, New York

1½ lb. GROUND BEEF
1 medium ONION, chopped
1 small GREEN PEPPER, chopped
1 10.5-oz. can BEEF BROTH
1 10.5-oz. can MUSHROOM SOUP
1 28-oz. can PORK & BEANS in TOMATO SAUCE
½ of 4-oz. can DICED GREEN CHILIS
10.5-oz. WATER
1 pkg. TACO SEASONING
Shredded CHEDDAR CHEESE
PARSLEY

In a large skillet brown beef. Add onion and green pepper . Cook until tender. Pour off excess fat. Add beef broth, mushroom soup, pork and beans, green chilies, water and taco seasoning. Mix well. Bring to a boil, reduce heat and simmer for 10 minutes, stirring occasionally. Spread cheese and parsley on top. This is a good leftover dish to heat up for lunch the next day.

Mexican Cornbread

1 8-oz. pkg. CORNBREAD MIX
¼ cup DRY MILK
½ cup WATER
1 EGG
½ of 4-oz. can DICED GREEN CHILIS
½ cup shredded MONTEREY JACK CHEESE

In a bowl combine cornbread mix and dry milk. Add water and egg. Mix well. Pour half of batter in 8" square pan. Sprinkle chilies and cheese over the batter. Cover with remaining batter. Bake 25 minutes in a 400-degree oven or until done. This can also be baked in a Dutch oven.

Pork Chops Mexicana

4 PORK CHOPS
1/3 cup OIL
1 medium-size ONION, chopped
1 small GREEN PEPPER, chopped
1 clove GARLIC, chopped
1 cup uncooked RICE
1 14.5-oz can MEXICAN DICED TOMATOES
½ cup BEEF BROTH
1 tsp. CHILI POWDER
SALT and PEPPER to taste

Brown both sides of chops in oil in a hot skillet. Remove chops to a baking pan. In the oil sauté onions, green pepper and garlic until lightly browned. Add rice and sauté until golden. Add tomatoes, broth and seasonings. Simmer for a minute to blend flavors. Pour over the chops. Cover and bake in a 325-degree oven for 1 hour. Remove cover the last 5 minutes to brown.

Breakfast Tortillas

Wrap scrambled eggs in tortillas for breakfast. Make the eggs with ham and cheese, salsa and chopped green pepper.

San Antonio Chilaqueiles

5 CORN TORTILLAS, cut in narrow strips
3 Tbsp. MARGARINE
½ medium ONION, chopped
1 4-oz. can DICED GREEN CHILIS
½ tsp. SALT
4 EGGS, slightly beaten
1 cup shredded CHEDDAR CHEESE
2 cups diced, cooked CHICKEN
SALSA

In a skillet fry tortilla chips in margarine until crisp. Add onion, chilies, salt and eggs. Cook until the eggs are partially set. Add cheese and chicken. Stir until eggs are set and chicken is hot. Serve topped with salsa.

South-of-the-Border Dressing

This recipe is a marinade as well as a dressing. Combine 2 cups of LIME JUICE, 3 Tbsp. RED WINE VINEGAR, ½ cup OLIVE OIL, and 2 Tbsp. dried RED PEPPER. Pour in a glass jar. Store in the refrigerator. When ready to use shake well.

Texas Cowboy Beans

2 lbs. PINTO BEANS
1 ONION, chopped
1 small piece SALT PORK
1 large clove GARLIC, crushed
½ tsp. CHILI POWDER
SALT and PEPPER to taste

Combine all ingredients in a Dutch oven. Have enough water to cover the beans by 3". Cook slowly until beans are soft, about 3 to 4 hours. Serve with steak or hamburgers.

Laredo Taco Peppers

1 lb. GROUND BEEF
1 pkg. TACO SEASONING
1 14.5-oz. can REFRIED BEANS
1 small ONION, chopped
1 cup CHUNKY SALSA
4 medium-size GREEN PEPPERS
1 medium-size TOMATO, CHOPPED
¼ cup shredded MONTEREY CHEESE
¼ cup shredded SHARP CHEDDAR CHEESE
½ cup SOUR CREAM

In a large skillet cook the ground beef. Drain the fat. Add taco seasoning, refried beans, onions and salsa. While the meat and bean mixture is heating thoroughly, cut the tops of the green peppers off. Remove seeds and stem. Immerse in boiling water for 3 minutes. Drain. Fill each pepper with the meat and bean mixture. Place in a 13"x9"x2" baking dish. Bake 20 minutes in a 350-degree oven or until the filling is cooked through. Cover with tomatoes, cheeses and sour cream.

Yucaipa Chicken Tacos

8 TACO SHELLS
4 cups cooked CHICKEN CHUNKS
1 4-oz. can DICED GREEN CHILIS
2 cups chopped ONION
2 cups shredded MONTEREY JACK CHEESE
2 cups cut-up TOMATOES
2 cups chopped LETTUCE
2 cups SALSA

Slightly heat taco shells. Divide the chicken chunks into the taco shells. Layer chilies, onion, cheese, and tomatoes one at a time over the chicken. Spread lettuce over all. Add salsa.

U is for Upside-Down Delights

Upside-Down Ham Loaf

2 lbs. GROUND HAM
½ cup MILK
1/8 tsp. PEPPER
2 EGGS, beaten
1 cup BREAD CRUMBS
1 20-oz. can CRUSHED PINEAPPLE

In a bowl combine everything but the pineapple. Mix thoroughly. Spread the pineapple at the bottom of a well-greased loaf pan. Spoon the ham mixture over the pineapple. Bake in a 350-degree oven for 1½ hours. Invert on a platter to serve.

Upside-Down Vegetable Pie

1 lb. pkg. frozen MIXED VEGETABLE
1 small ONION, chopped
½ of the WATER from cooked vegetables
2 Tbsp. MARGARINE
1 Tbsp. KETCHUP
1 cup BAKING MIX
2 Tbsp. SHORTENING
1 EGG
½ cup MILK
1 10.5-oz. can MUSHROOM SOUP

Cook vegetables with the onions following package instructions.

Add the vegetable water, margarine and ketchup. Heat for10 minutes. Pour into a 2-quart casserole dish. In a bowl stir the baking mix with shortening. Add egg and milk. Pour the batter over the vegetables. Bake in a 400-degree oven for a half hour. Turn out inverted on a heated serving dish. Heat the mushroom soup and serve over the vegetables.

Georgia Peach Upside-Down Cake

¼ cup MARGARINE
½ cup BROWN SUGAR
1 15-oz. can PEACHES
CROUTONS
1 tsp. CINNAMON
1 tsp. SUGAR

In the bottom of a heated Dutch oven, stir the margarine and brown sugar together until the margarine is melted. Arrange the peaches evenly over the margarine and sugar. Put a thick layer of croutons

over the fruit. Mix and spread the cinnamon and sugar over the croutons. Sprinkle some of the peach juice over all. Cover and bake until the peaches are bubbly and the croutons are brown. This could also be cooked in a pan in a 350-degree oven.

Upside-Down Chocolate Cake

1 DEVILS FOOD CAKE MIX
EGG
MILK
2 cups MINI MARSHMALLOWS
1 cup BROWN SUGAR
½ cup COCOA
2 cups HOT WATER
1 cup chopped WALNUTS

Make the cake batter according to directions on the package using the egg and milk. Spread the marshmallows evenly on the bottom of a 13"x9"x2" baking dish. Combine brown sugar, cocoa and water. Pour over marshmallows. Spoon cake batter over the marshmallows. Top with walnuts. Bake in a 350-degree oven for 45-50 minutes. Remove from oven. Turn out inverted on a platter.

Upside-Down Pear Gingerbread

¼ cup MARGARINE
1/3 cup BROWN SUFAR
1 15-oz. can PEAR HALVES
1 box GINGERBREAD MIX
WHIPPED CREAM

Stir and melt the margarine in an oblong baking pan with the brown sugar. Drain the juice of the pears. Place the pears cut-side down on the brown sugar. Mix the gingerbread according to directions on package. Pour over the pears. Bake in a 350-degree oven until done. Turn out on serving plate, fruit side up. Serve with whipped cream. Sliced tart apples can also be used.

Upside-Down Frankfurters

½ cup chopped ONION
½ cup chopped GREEN PEPPER
OIL
1 15-oz. can STEWED TOMATOES
1 Tbsp. SWEET PICKLE RELISH
½ tsp. MUSTARD
SALT and PEPPER to taste
1 pkg. CORNBREAD MUFFIN MIX
8 FRANKFURTERS

Sauté onions and green pepper in oil until tender. Stir in tomatoes, relish and seasoning. Heat while making the cornbread batter according to package directions. Arrange frankfurters at the bottom of a baking dish. Slit diagonally along the backs of each. Cover with tomato mixture. Spoon cornbread over tomatoes. Bake in a 400-degree oven for 20-25 minutes or until cornbread is done. Let cool 5 minutes. Loosen around edges before inverting onto a platter. This recipe could also be used with cooked ground beef.

*Cube turkey ham to use in any favorite ham recipes.

V is for Vegetables

Outback-Grilled Veggies

Submitted by Wanda Smith, Lake Havasu City, Arizona

1 large GREEN PEPPER
1 large RED PEPPER
1 large YELLOW PEPPER
2 ZUCCHINI
2 cups MUSHROOMS
1 medium RED ONION
1 cup BRUSSELS SPROUTS
OLIVE or CANOLA OIL
GARLIC SALT and PEPPER to taste

Clean, cut and slice all the vegetables. Place them in a plastic bag. Spray the oil on the veggies in the bag. Add seasoning. Mix veggies with the oil and seasonings. Keep in bag until ready to grill. Place veggies in a large piece of foil and wrap securely. Place on grill. Cook to desired tenderness.

Oven Vegetables

Submitted by Esther Chumbley, Lake Havasu City, Arizona

"This is a quick, no fuss dish."

10-oz. pkg. frozen MIXED VEGETABLES
2 Tbsp. BUTTER or MARGARINE
2 Tbsp. WATER
½ tsp. SALT
½ tsp. DILL WEED

Mix all the ingredients in a 4-cup casserole dish. Cover and bake in a 325-degree oven for 30 minutes or until done. Stir once to blend.

*TO COOK VEGETABLES: Allow the shortest possible time to cook vegetables. The shorter the time, the more delicious they are.

Fried Cucumbers

1½ lbs. CUCUMBER
2 EGGS
SALT to taste
½ cup BREAD CRUMBS or
1 cup crushed CORN FLAKES
OIL

Peel cucumbers and slice ¼" thick. Beat eggs and seasoning in a small bowl. Dip cucumber slices in egg mixture, then in crumbs or crushed flakes. Heat oil in large skillet. Fry cucumber slices a few at a time, about 2 minutes on each side. Drain on paper towels.

Mixed Veggie Salad

1 10-oz. pkg. frozen MIXED VEGETABLES
1 15-oz. can KIDNEY BEANS, rinsed and drained
½ cup chopped ONION
½ cup chopped CELERY
½ cup chopped GREEN PEPPER
¾ cup SUGAR
½ cup RED WINE VINEGAR
1 Tbsp. CORNSTARCH

Cook vegetables until tender. Drain. Place in a large bowl. Add kidney beans, onion, celery and green pepper. In a saucepan cook sugar, vinegar and cornstarch until thickened. Cool. Pour over vegetables. Toss until all vegetables are coated. Chill.

Vegetable Medley

For each serving put a slice of TOMATO, some peeled and cubed EGGPLANT, thin slice of RED ONION, slices of MUSHROOM, a few frozen PEAS, and a pat of BUTTER in a large piece of foil. Sprinkle with WATER and SALT and PEPPER to taste. Wrap tightly. Grill for 15 minutes, turning once.

Cheesy Broccoli Soup

Submitted by Logan Dean, Brodhead, Wisconsin

2 cups WATER
2 CHICKEN BOUILLON CUBES
1 10-oz. pkg. frozen BROCCOLI
3 cups MILK
½ cup shredded CHEDDAR CHEESE
½ cup FLOUR
¼ cup WATER

In a saucepan combine water, bouillon cubes and broccoli. Cook until tender. Add milk and cheese. Mix and cook together water and flour until thickened. Add to soup. Bring all to boil. Cool.

Red Cabbage in Wine

3 strips BACON, cut into small pieces
1 medium ONION, sliced
½ cup RED WINE VINEGAR
½ cup WATER
2½-3 lbs. RED CABBAGE, chopped
½ GREEN APPLE, chopped
1 tsp. each SALT and SUGAR
PEPPER to taste

Cook bacon and onion together in a large pan to brown. Add vinegar and water Add remaining ingredients. Cover and simmer until cabbage is tender about 30 minutes.

Old-Fashioned Glazed Onions

Cook 3 cups small, silver-skinned ONIONS in salted boiling water for 15 minutes. Drain. Dry on paper towels. Melt 3 Tbsp. BUTTER in a skillet. Add 2 Tbsp. SUGAR and onions. Gently cook until brown. If necessary, to prevent burning, use mat under skillet.

Grilled Vegetables

Submitted by Lewis Dean Clark, Camerillo, California

In a large piece of aluminum foil wrap pats of butter, favorite seasoning and enough corn-on-the-cob for your group, or a whole head of cauliflower, enough carrots or broccoli for the group, peas, a whole eggplant, string beans, whole zucchini, whatever. Clean and prepare the vegetable you are having for dinner. Wipe dry. Put the vegetable-stuffed foil piece by the side of the campfire. Turn now and then to get all the sides cooked. This is an easy, delicious and succulent way to have vegetables when camping.

Korean Salad

1 lb. fresh SPINACH
½ lb. fresh BEAN SPROUTS
½ 8-oz. can WATER CHESTNUTS, sliced
2 HARD-COOKED EGGS, chopped
6 slices BACON, cooked and crumbled

In a large bowl combine washed and cleaned spinach and bean sprouts. Add the water chestnuts, eggs and bacon. Make the dressing (below). Toss well to cover the salad.

Korean Dressing

½ cup PEANUT OIL
1/3 cup SUGAR
1/3 cup KETCHUP
¼ cup VINEGAR
1 tsp. PAPRIKA
1 tsp. A-I SAUCE
½ small ONION, grated
1 Tbsp. BRANDY

Mix all ingredients. Refrigerate any leftover dressing.

Shenandoah Succotash

2 Tbsp. BUTTER
¼ cup finely chopped RED PEPPER
1 Tbsp. finely sliced CELERY
1 14.5-oz. can CORN, drained
1 14.5-oz. can BABY GREEN LIMA BEANS, drained
SALT and PEPPER to taste
½ of 4-oz. can MUSHROOMS
½ cup MILK

In a saucepan melt butter. Saute red pepper and celery until tender. Add remaining ingredients. Heat until hot and well blended.

Peas with Celery and Mushrooms

1 cup finely chopped CELERY
1 10.5-oz. can CHICKEN BROTH
2 cups FROZEN PEAS
1 4-oz can MUSHROOMS
SALT and PEPPER to taste

Cook celery in chicken broth over medium heat 10 minutes. Add peas, mushrooms and seasoning. Reduce heat and simmer 5 to 8 minutes or until peas are tender.

Cabbage and Sour Cream

1 head CABBAGE, shredded
1 EGG, beaten
2 Tbsp. SUGAR
SALT to taste
1 cup SOUR CREAM

Boil the cabbage about 5 minutes or until tender. Drain. Add remaining ingredients, one at a time. Cook over low heat until cooked through.

W is for Water Camping, Rafting and Houseboating

Many people are finding river rafting and "camping" in a houseboat or a 'party-boat' on a lake very enjoyable. Camping on the banks of a river or floating lazily on a lake takes as much preparation as backpacking in the mountains. Read O is for ON-THE-TRAIL chapter for ideas. Careful planning is important to insure a safe and comfortable experience and to meet the needs of the environment.

Familiarize yourself with the water way you are going to visit. Know the climate you might experience, type of country you will see, the wildlife you may meet and the services available.

Rafting

Professional rafting guides pack daily all-inclusive containers. On sandbars and riverbanks, where they camp, boxes are well organized to fit the needs of a day. Plan the length of time your trip will take, and the number of people who will be aboard. If it is just for the day make some tempting sandwiches, (well wrapped so they do not become soaked.) Take fruit, cookies and juice. An outing such as rafting makes one very hungry. Chocolate or granola bars are great snacks. For an extended trip plan menus and quantity of food to fit the group. Plan for an extra day in case of emergency.

Houseboats and Party-Boats

There is more flexibility in what you take in a houseboat as you live or 'camp' in the boat and not on a sandbar as in rafting. Plan the trip to fit the size of the group who will be aboard. You can cook good meals on a one-burner stove and hibachi. It just takes careful planning. However, on research, some houseboats are 60' long, deluxe camping units equipped with ovens, stoves, disposals, dish washers like a large motor home. All you need to take is food and drink. Parties usually rent the houseboats for a minimum of three nights.

Party-boaters camp on the shores of the lake or river. There are campgrounds reached only by boat for boaters. Like camping in the mountains, everything you take in must come out.

Keep the pantry items in one box so it is clean and easy to transport. Pack the pots, dishes, silverware, napkins, foil etc. together. As in mountain backpacking, prepare foods at home, to eliminate the waste of the preparation at camp. Waste is essential to consider. Liquids can be dumped in the lake or river, but no food should be thrown in the water. Keep burnable refuse in plastic bags to dispose of when on shore. Keep garbage foods, foil and crushed cans in containers to dispose of on shore.

Helpful Hints In Planning

1. Plan simple, varied meals.
2. Prepare fruits and vegetables at home to minimize waste. Store food in plastic bags.
3. For a special treat use rolls and exotic breads.
4. Cook hamburger meat at home. Freeze it, as it will last a few days after defrosting in the ice chest.
5. Render bacon and sausages at home, freeze and reheat at camp.
6. Keep eggs in the plastic egg container so they do not break.
7. Store the hibachi on the boat away from the compass board.
8. Have a fire extinguisher handy when cooking on board.
9. Start a meal with a hot cup of canned soup.
10. Make cole slaw, potato salad and deviled eggs at home. Pack in plastic containers.
11. Make sandwiches at breakfast to be ready for lunch.
12. Crush cans flat to minimize trash space.
13. Use paper plates that can be burned.
14. Take enough liquids—bottled water, fruit juices and sodas as well as coffee and tea.
15. Take fruit, cheese and crackers for snacks.
16. Make sure life jackets are in good condition.
17. Plan for an extra day in case of emergency.

X is for X-tra Goodies

Bread Loaf

An old-timer told me what he used to do when he went fishing.

Take a loaf of bread—sourdough, sheepherders, or French and cut a thick slab of the crust off at one end. Scoop out the soft center leaving about an inch shell. Save the bread from the center for crumbs, mix with herbs and store for future use.

Make your favorite meatloaf, using some of the crumbs from the center. Melt 2 Tbsp. BUTTER in a saucepan. Add about ½ tsp. each of PARSLEY, THYME, GARLIC SALT, PEPPER and ONION POWDER. Add 1 tsp. prepared MUSTARD and ½ tsp. WORCESTERSHIRE SAUCE. Mix well. Brush the inside of the shell with this sauce.

Mix the meatloaf with your hands. Stuff the meatloaf mixture inside the bread shell. Using the bread crust that was cut off as a lid, toothpick it into place. Brush the loaf with milk. Wrap the loaf in foil. Bake in a 350-degree oven for 1 ½ hours. Cool before cutting into thick slabs. Wrap individually in foil. Send the fishermen out to the lake and if they don't catch any fish, at least they won't starve.

Beef Heart

Submitted by Phil Dirks, Lake Havasu City, Arizona

Soak a beef heart in cold water overnight. Right after breakfast, open the cavity of the beef heart. Fill the cavity with some cut-up onions, green peppers, celery, clove of garlic, and anything else you like. Wrap the heart in 2 layers of foil. Put on a bed of coals in a hole where the fire was built. Cover with more coals. Fill the balance of hole with dirt. Go on a hike or fish all day. It will be ready upon your return in the afternoon.

Fudge

On a rainy day or just when your sweet tooth speaks up, make a batch of fudge. Kids love to make it as well as consume it.

1 cup SEMI-SWEET CHOCOLATE CHIPS
1 12-oz. can SWEET CONDENSED MILK
1 Tbsp. BUTTER
½ tsp. VANILLA
1 cup CHOPPED nuts

Melt chips over hot water. Stir until smooth. Add milk. Cook 10 minutes or to the soft ball stage, stirring frequently. Remove from the heat. Add butter. Pour into an 8" square pan. Let stand to cool.

Additional Ideas for Fudge

1. Before pouring into an 8" square pan add 12 small marshmallows. Cut into pieces with wet scissors. Cool. Cut into squares.

2. Before pouring into the pan add ½ to 1 cup of chopped peanuts, walnuts or pecans to the mixture. Cool. Cut into squares.

3. Pour half of fudge into the pan. Sprinkle a layer of peanut butter chips over it. Cover with rest of fudge. Cool. Cut into squares.

Brownsville Brown Sugar Squares

2 cups packed BROWN SUGAR
¾ cup CREAM
¼ tsp. SALT
2 Tbsp. BUTTER
¾ cup chopped NUTS
1 tsp. VANILLA

Dissolve brown sugar in the cream. Add salt. Cook until the soft ball stage tested in cold water. Remove from heat. Add butter, nuts and vanilla. Cool. Beat until creamy. Press into 8" square pan. Cut into squares.

Dean's Homemade Oreo Cookies

Submitted by Paige and Matthew Dean, Greer, South Carolina

1 pkg. DEVILS FOOD CAKE MIX
2/3 cups CRISCO
2 EGGS, beaten
WHITE FROSTING

Mix all ingredients together except the frosting. Mix until smooth. Shape into 1" balls. Flatten with the bottom of a glass dipped in sugar. Place on a cookie sheet. Bake in a 350-degree oven for 8 to 10 minutes. Put together as a sandwich with the frosting.

Raisin Sauce for Pork

1½ cup APPLE JUICE
1½ cup RAISINS
½ cup MAPLE SYRUP
½ tsp. GROUND CINNAMON
1 tsp. CORNSTARCH
2 Tbsp. COLD WATER

Heat to boil apple juice, raisins, maple syrup and cinnamon. Reduce heat and simmer until raisins are tender. Mix cornstarch and water. Boil together to thicken for 1 minute. Add to raisins.

Taos Salsa Bread

1 cup shredded MONTEREY JACK CHEESE
¾ cup CHUNKY SALSA or
PICANTE SAUCE
1 large CHEESE-FLAVORED PIZZA CRUST

Mix together ½ of the cheese and all of the salsa. Spread over the pizza crust. Top with rest of cheese. Put in pizza pan. Bake in 350-degree oven until cheese is melted. Cut into wedges. Great with soup.

Y is for Yams

Yams and sweet potatoes are quite similar. However, not only is the color different, but yams are much sweeter, less fat and juicier than sweet potatoes. Some people prefer yams to sweet potatoes for the taste as well as the color. They can be used and prepared the same way in cooking.

Yummy Yams Gratin

1½ lbs. YAMS
2 Tbsp. BUTTER
½ cup VEGETABLE BROTH
2 Tbsp. MAPLE SYRUP
1 Tbsp. LIME JUICE
SALT and PEPPER to taste

Wash and prick whole yams. Place on an ungreased baking sheet. Bake until tender, about an hour. Cool to touch. Peel and mash potatoes in a large bowl into chunky pieces. Mix in the butter. Add the broth, maple syrup, lime juice and seasoning, mashing into a puree. Pour the mixture into a greased 9" pie dish. Bake in a 350-degree oven for 30 to 40 minutes or until lightly brown.

Yam Salad

4 medium YAMS
4 GREEN ONIONS, chopped
1 cup chopped CELERY
2 HARD-COOKED EGGS, mashed
½ cup MAYONNAISE
½ cup FRENCH DRESSING
SALT and PEPPER to taste

Cook, peel and mash the yams. Place in a bowl. Mix in the rest of the remaining ingredients. Let stand and chill thoroughly.

Yams with Apples

Butter the bottom of a Dutch oven. Arrange cooked and sliced YAMS in layers with 3 tart, peeled and sliced APPLES. Sprinkle BROWN SUGAR and CINNAMON on each layer. Cook 30 minutes. Serve with your favorite sausages or pork chops.

Bourbon Mashed Yams

2 lbs. YAMS, cooked, peeled and mashed
½ cup HEAVY CREAM
1/3 cup KENTUCKY BOURBON
3 Tbsp. BROWN SUGAR
2 Tbsp. MOLASSES
1/8 tsp. SALT

Prepare yams. Add remaining ingredients. Beat until well blended. Keep warm. Serve with glazed baby carrots.

Georgian Yams

Place 3 cups of cooked, mashed YAMS in a buttered baking dish. Heat 2 Tbsp. MOLASSES and 1 Tbsp. of BUTTER in a saucepan until the butter is melted. Pour over the yams and bake in a 350-degree oven for 30 minutes or until they are brown and bubbly.

Yam-Stuffed Green Peppers

2 GREEN PEPPERS, cut in half lengthwise
¼ cup MARGARINE
½ of 4-oz. can MUSHROOMS
½ cup chopped ONIONS
1 16-oz. can YAMS, drained and mashed
2 slices BACON, cooked and crumbled
1 EGG, beaten
SALT and PEPPER to taste

Remove the seeds and fiber from green peppers. Rinse. Cook in boiling water for 5 minute. Drain. In a skillet melt the margarine. Sauté the mushrooms and onions. Add yams, bacon, egg, and seasoning. Blend thoroughly. Put in green pepper shells. Bake in a shallow pan in a 350-degree oven for 30 minutes.

Georgian Fried Sweet Potatoes

Cut cooked SWEET POTATOES in strips lengthwise. Fry the potatoes in deep MARGARINE to a golden brown. Drain on paper towels. Sprinkle SALT and PEPPER to taste on top.

Sherried Sweet Potatoes

2 lbs. SWEET POTATOES
1/3 cup MARGARINE
¼ cup SHERRY or ORANGE JUICE
1/3 tsp. ORANGE ZEST
Pinch of NUTMEG
Pinch of CINNAMON
SALT and PEPPER to taste
BROWN SUGAR

Boil the potatoes, unpeeled, for 20 minutes or until almost tender. Peel and mash. Mix with margarine. Add flavoring, spices and seasoning. Whip until the potato mixture is fluffy. If the mixture is too dry, add a little of the water from cooking. Place in a shallow baking pan. Sprinkle with brown sugar. Bake in a 400-degree oven long enough to get the top lightly browned.

Merrivale Hashed Sweet Potatoes

Mix 2 cups cooked, mashed SWEET POTATOES with ONION POWDER, SALT and PEPPER and ½ cup leftover chopped TURKEY or HAM. Brown slowly in oil on one side, turn and brown on the other. Sprinkle with parsley.

Z is for Zucchini

Fried Zucchini

3 medium ZUCCHINI, washed and scrubbed
Hot OLIVE OIL
SALT and PEPPER to taste
1 Tbsp. finely chopped PARSLEY
2 Tbsp. grated PARMESAN CHEESE

Slice the zucchini crosswise into 2" pieces. Sauté in hot oil until lightly browned on both sides. Sprinkle seasoning on top. Mix parsley and cheese together. Spread on top while still hot.

Stuffed Zucchini

1 lb. GROUND BEEF
½ small ONION, chopped
½ tsp. minced GARLIC
¼ cup thinly sliced CELERY
½ of 4-oz. can of MUSHROOMS
1 cup cooked RICE
1 EGG
1 4-oz. can TOMATO SAUCE
SALT and PEPPER to taste
2 large ZUCCHINI
½ cup shredded MONTEREY JACK CHEESE

Brown beef, onion, garlic and celery. Add mushrooms, rice, egg, tomato sauce and seasoning. Cut zucchini lengthwise. Scope out pulp to make shells. Add pulp to meat mixture. Stuff zucchini. Spread cheese on top. Bake in a 350-degree oven for 1 hour.

Grilled Zucchini

Cut 2 small ZUCCHINI in quarters. Add SASONING and LEMON JUICE on top. Wrap pieces in foil. Grill 12-14 minutes.

Zucchini Bread

Submitted by Linda Dean, Brodhead, Wisconsin

3 EGGS, beaten
1 cup OIL
2 cups SUGAR
3 cups FLOUR
1 3 tsp. CINNAMON
1 tsp. SALT
1 tsp. BAKING SODA
½ tsp. BAKING POWDER
2 cups grated ZUCCHINI
1 tsp. VANILLA

Combine all the ingredients. Add raisins or nuts if desired. Pour into well-greased and floured loaf pan. Bake in a 350-degree oven for approximately 1 hour.

Altoona Stuffed Jumbo Zucchini

1 large ZUCCHINI
SALT to taste
2 cups HERBED BREAD CRUMBS
½ cup finely chopped ONION
½ of 4-oz. can MUSHROOMS
4 Tbsp. BUTTER melted in ¼ cup WATER
1 EGG, slightly beaten
½ chopped CELERY
½ cup slivered ALMONDS, optional

Clean zucchini. Cut off ends and split lengthwise. Remove seeds and pulp. Sprinkle with salt. Combine pulp with bread crumbs, onions, mushrooms, butter, water and egg. Add celery and almonds. Toss lightly. Fill the zucchini shells. Wrap each half in foil. Grill over coals for 30 to 35 minutes or until tender.

Zucchini Bake

Submitted by Elizabeth Gattenby, Lake Havasu City, Arizona

1 stick BUTTER, cut in small pieces
4 large ZUCCHINI, sliced crosswise ¼" thick
6 sliced fresh MUSHROOMS
½ finely chopped sweet ONION
2 cups crushed SODA CRACKER CRUMBS
½ tsp. GARLIC POWDER
½ tsp. dried DILL WEED
SCALDED MILK

Layer all ingredients, except milk, in a baking dish. Pour enough milk to just moisten, not throughout the mixture. Do not pour to the top. Bake in a 375-degree oven for an hour.

Broiled Zucchini

Wash 2 lbs. zucchini. Cut ends and slice lengthwise. Brush with melted butter, salt and pepper. Broil 5" to 6" from heat, 10 to 12 minutes or until tender.

Zucchini Salmon Bake For Two

ZUCCHINI for two, sliced
2 SALMON STEAKS
6 medium MUSHROOMS, sliced
1 cup MILK
1 egg, BEATEN
½ cup PARMESAN CHEESE

Arrange zucchini at the bottom of a buttered baking dish. Lay salmon steaks on top. Place mushrooms on top of steaks. Mix milk, egg and cheese together. Pour over steaks and zucchini. Bake in 350-degree oven for 35-40 minutes or until fish flakes. This recipe is good with any firm fish like halibut, swordfish or sea bass.

PS is for Picnics and Sandwiches

Lunch is the perfect time to have a picnic—to sit in a town park under a shade tree, to look at a mountain view beside a gurgling stream or a colorful mountain beside a tawny silt-strewn river… a balmy beach with breakers dashing up the sand. Pack a hamper and take in the view. It is a chance to get out of the car or motor vehicle and feel different environs and places.

Keep a hamper equipped with clean paper plates, cups, napkins, paper towels, plastic utensils and a colorful tablecloth. Have an ice chest full of delectable sandwiches, fruit, juices, cookies and a small candy bar to satisfy that sweet tooth. Small jars of pickles and olives enhance the menu. Kids love potato and corn chips. Clean the hamper out at night to prepare for the next day.

Fruits that hold up are apples, plums, bananas, and grapes. Oranges can be messy eating with dripping juices. Peaches squish and tend to get sloppy as some varieties are very soft and pulpy.

If the ice chest is big enough take along a cole slaw, potato or macaroni salad, hard-cooked eggs, eggplant salad. Sample various types of cheese not usually eaten or used at home. Make it a fun adventure. Try different crackers and wafers to eat with the cheese. And, if the weather is chilly, what is better than a thermos with hot soup or chowder to go with the crackers and cheese?

Some take-alongs to go with sandwiches are lettuce leaves, sliced or cherry tomatoes, carrot or celery sticks, sliced cucumbers, green pepper strips, olives, pickles and pickled onions.

There are interesting breads like pita, Italian, French, sourdough, dark and light rye, pumpernickel, whole or 12-grain, cornbread, rolls or tortillas. (One idea is to slit lengthwise a loaf of Italian or French bread and stuff it with leftover meat loaf, salami, ham or turkey with interesting cheeses or salad and slice it into thick slabs for individual servings.)

Ideas For Sandwiches

1. Corned beef with mustard, slices of red onion and alfalfa sprouts.
2. Smoked salmon with cheese.
3. Salami or liverwurst with hard-cooked eggs.
4. Tomato slices with sharp cheddar cheese and crisp bacon.
5. Roast beef with potato salad.
6. Pressed or red caviar with red onion and egg slices.
7. Canned shrimp or crabmeat with parsley in a salad.
8. Cream cheese with green and red pepper finely chopped.
9. Smoked tongue with thin slices of white chicken meat.
10. Roquefort cheese, chopped chicken meat and crumbled bacon.
11. Hard-cooked eggs with prosciutto and chopped pickles.
12. Hard-cooked eggs with crumbled bacon and chopped onion.
13. Minced tuna with horseradish, cream cheese and lemon juice.
14. Mashed baked beans with chopped onions and frankfurters.
15. Chopped ham, celery, apple or pineapple with salad dressing.
16. Mortedello with slices of hard-cooked eggs.

Always butter both slices of bread. It insulates the bread from the filling keeping the bread from getting soggy. Less mayonnaise is needed, which has lower fat content.

Interesting Butters for Spreading:

Use ¼ lb. of butter:

1. Add 1 tsp. Dijon mustard with 1 tsp. dry mustard or 2 tsp. mild prepared mustard.
2. Add 2 cloves of garlic, mashed.
3. Add 3 coarsely chopped anchovy fillets.
4. Add1½ Tbsp. chopped chutney.
5. Add to softened butter 2 tsp. fresh grated horseradish. This is especially delicious with roast beef sandwiches.

6. Add 5-6 finely chopped shrimp, with salt and pepper to taste.

7. Add 1 Tbsp. chopped capers.

8. Add 3 finely chopped shallots.

9. Add1½ tsp. dry tarragon rubbed to a powder with the hands.

10. Add 2 Tbsp. mashed sardines with a touch of lemon juice.

Another kind of picnic is to cook hamburgers, hot dogs, sausages or steaks, chicken, fish and seafood on the grill. Forget the sandwiches. It will make a more leisurely picnic by cooking the meat. Take buns or rolls with other fixings like salsa, relish, ketchup, mustard and pickles. Many town parks have picnic areas with barbecue stands for you to use with your coals. Or, carry a small hibachi, Weber cooker or gas grill with you. Prepare hamburger patties or whatever meat you are going to cook before you go on the picnic.

Xtra special ideas to take on a picnic:

Round Celery Sticks

In a bowl mix together 3-oz. CREAM CHEESE, 3 Tbsp. BUTTER and 2 tsp. ANCHOVY PASTE. In another bowl mix 3-oz. BLEU CHEESE and 3 Tbsp. BUTTER together. Put the anchovy-cream cheese mixture on 12 4" pieces of celery sticks and 12 4" pieces of celery sticks with blue cheese mixture. Press the two together to make a round. Refrigerate in plastic bags.

Meatballs

With your favorite meatloaf recipe shape the meat into tiny balls with your hands. Cook in hot olive oil slowly until done, about 5 minutes, turning to cook evenly. Cool and wrap in foil or plastic bags and refrigerate. Unwrap and eat cold on the picnic.

Walnut Sticks

Cut crusts from 12 white bread slices. Cut into 1" wide strips. Blend 8-oz. CREAM CHEESE, 1 Tbsp. CREAM, ½ tsp. CURRY POWDER, ½ tsp. LEMON JUICE and 1 cup finely chopped WALNUTS. Blend everything together except the walnuts. Spread cheese mixture on both sides of bread. Dip and press walnuts into the cheese. Wrap between layers of wax paper or plastic to store.

Jazzy Potato Salad

1 ½ lbs. RED POTATOES
SALTED WATER
½ cup WHITE WINE
½ cup OIL
¼ cup VINEGAR
SALT and PEPPER to taste
½ cup finely chopped ONION
½ cup thinly sliced CELERY
½ tsp. chopped fresh PARSLEY

Boil POTATOES in SALTED WATER until just soft. Pour cold water over them. Peel at once. Cut them in halves or quarters. Add WINE and more SALT, if necessary. Let marinate for 30 minutes, stirring occasionally. In a bowl mix the remaining ingredients. Toss well. Add POTATOES. Blend. Pack in a plastic bowl, cover with foil and carry in the cooler for the picnic.

Crunchy Chicken Salad

3 cups diced cooked CHICKEN
1 cup thinly sliced CELERY
1 tsp. finely chopped ONION
2/3 cup MAYONNAISE
1 Tbsp. RED WINE VINEGAR
SALT and PEPPER to taste
CHICKEN SEASONING to taste
¼ cup coarsely chopped PECANS
¼ cup sliced SPANISH OLIVES

In a mixing bowl combine CHICKEN, CELERY and ONION. In another bowl mix together MAYONNAISE, VINEGAR and SEASONINGS. Add more MAYONNAISE if necesary. Add CHOPPED PECANS and OLIVE SLICES as a decoration around the salad bowl. For an added touch, serve tips of asparagus and peach halves filled with cottage cheese and parsley.

ORDER BLANK

GOLDEN WEST PUBLISHERS

4113 N. Longview Ave. • Phoenix, AZ 85014

www.goldenwestpublishers.com • 1-800-658-5830 • FAX 602-279-6901

Qty	Title	Price	Amount
	ABC's of Camp Cooking	9.95	
	Arizona Cook Book	6.95	
	Best Barbecue Recipes	6.95	
	Burrito Lovers Cook Book	6.95	
	Chili-Lovers' Cook Book	6.95	
	Chip and Dip Lovers Cook Book	6.95	
	Cowboy Cartoon Cookbook	7.95	
	Gourmet Gringo Cook Book	14.95	
	Kokopelli's Cook Book	9.95	
	Low Fat Mexican Recipes	6.95	
	Mexican Desserts & Drinks	6.95	
	New Mexico Cook Book	6.95	
	Quick-n-Easy Mexican Recipes	6.95	
	Real New Mexico Chile	6.95	
	Salsa Lovers Cook Book	6.95	
	Take This Chile & Stuff It!	6.95	
	Tequila Cook Book	7.95	
	Tortilla Lovers Cook Book	6.95	
	Vegi-Mex: Vegetarian Mexican Recipes	6.95	
	Western Breakfasts	7.95	

U.S. Shipping & Handling Add: 1-3 Books $5.00
(Shipping to all other countries see website.) 4+ Books $7.00

Arizona residents add 8.1% sales tax

Total $________
(Payable in U.S. funds)

☐ My Check or Money Order Enclosed

☐ MasterCard ☐ VISA ☐ Discover ☐ American Express

Acct. No. ____________________ Exp. Date __________

Signature ______________________________

Name ____________________ Phone __________

Address ______________________________

City/State/Zip ______________________________

06/06 **Call for a FREE catalog of all of our titles**

GOLDEN WEST PUBLISHERS

If you love cookbooks, then you'll love these too!

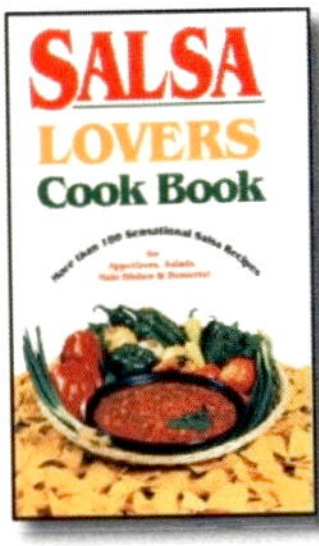

More than 180 recipes for salsa, dips, salads, appetizers and more!
$9.95

Make your favorite Mexican dishes in record time! Excellent tacos, tostadas, enchiladas and more!
$9.95

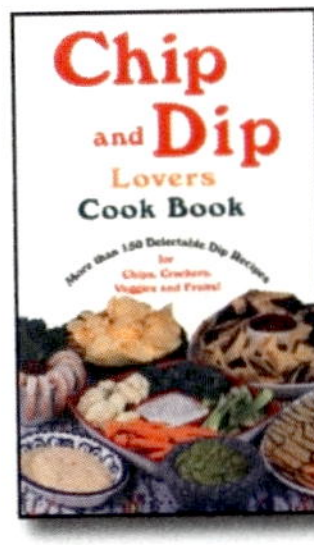

Easy and colorful recipes from Southwestern salsas to quick appetizer dips!
$9.95

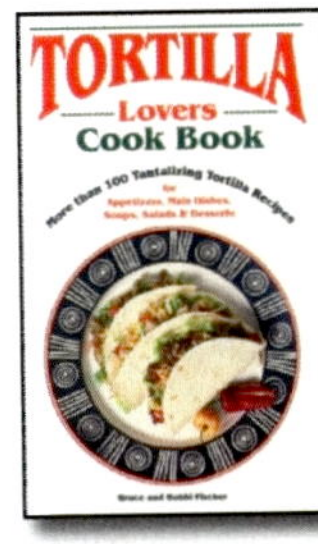

Celebrate the tortilla with more than 100 easy recipes for breakfast, lunch, dinner, and desserts!
$9.95

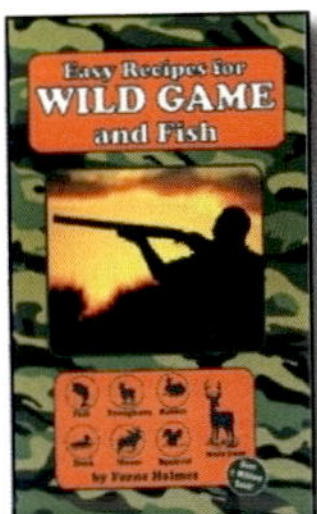

More than 200 "wild" recipes for large and small game, wild fowl and fish.
$9.95

A collection of authentic Arizona recipes. Including Indian, Mexican, and Western foods.
$9.95

This unique book explores the age-old recipes that are rich with the heritage of New Mexico.
$6.95

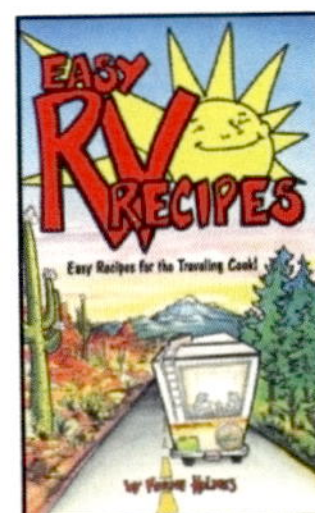

Easy recipes for the traveling cook. Over 200 recipes to make in your RV, camper, or houseboat.
$9.95

Prize-winning recipes for chili, with or without beans. Plus taste-tempting foods made with flavorful chile peppers.
$9.95

What's more American than eating apple pie? Over 150 favorite recipes for appetizers, main and side dishes, pies, beverages, and preserves.
$9.95

Over 175 recipes for soups, breads, muffins, pies, cakes, cheesecakes, cookies, and even ice cream! Carving tips, trivia, and more.
$9.95

250 authentic, home-style recipes for tacos, tamales, menudo, enchiladas, burros, salsas, chile rellenos, guacamole, and more!
$9.95

www.goldenwestpublishers.com

Cookbooks USA

For Cookbook Lovers of all ages!

Have you been to the ultimate cooking website yet?!

At **Cookbooks USA** you'll find a cookbook for every occasion and palate. Over 20 recipe categories to choose from and enjoy. BBQ, Desserts, Famous Chefs, Holidays, Regional and Southwestern are just a few.

But **Cookbooks USA** is more than cookbooks! It's food fun, with Celebrity Cookbook Reviews, Weird & Wacky recipes, Community Food Events and best of all, the first ever **Cookbook-A-Month Gift Package Program**! No club to join or extra books to buy – just great cooking with a new cookbook delivered to your doorstep every month. What a terrific gift!

You'll even find grandma back in the kitchen with the "*Grandma's Favorite ...*" series.

From free recipes to Fundraising with Cookbooks and a *Fun, Friendly & Free Monthly Foodletter*, discover a whole new world of cooking and food enjoyment at **Cookbooks USA.**

Mmmmmm! Good things are cookin' at

www.cookbooksusa.com